Papa Floribunda

Papa Floribunda

A Biography of
Eugene S. Boerner

By Robert W. Wells

ISBN 0-9621813-0-7

Library of Congress Catalog Card No. 88-63976

© Copyright 1989

BBG Publishing Company
c/o Bank I Trust Company NA
111 East Wisconsin Avenue
Milwaukee, Wisconsin 53202

Printed in the United States of America
C.W. Brown Printing Co.
Oconomowoc, Wisconsin

Eugene S. Boerner hybridizing roses.

Table of Contents

Foreword

Eugene S. Boerner was an internationally-known rose hybridizer who died in 1966 at the age of seventy-three. To him, hybridizing was a field of romantic exploration, a chance to improve on nature by the cunning of man, an exploration in which the perfect rose might be found by luck and intuition as much as by research and design. That was the romance of the game, the dramatic suspense, "that on any dewy morning a miracle might occur...."

This book is the story of his life. From other perspectives, however, it is also the story of a German family that came to the United States in 1837 to settle in Cedarburg, Wisconsin; of international efforts by a small number of men in Germany, Italy, France, Spain, Ireland, England and the United States to improve and market roses; of Nazi Germany before World War II and the saving of at least some of Europe's roses; and, finally, of the role Boerner played in establishing the floribunda rose as a variety of its own which captured the American market.

Most of the details in this book have not been published before. Boerner's work has been built upon by a new generation of rose hybridizers who know very little of him except for the legacy of improved varieties he left behind. To them, the gardener, the horticulturist and perhaps the historian, this book should be of particular interest.

The manuscript for *Papa Floribunda* was written by Robert W. Wells shortly after Boerner's death, based upon the mountain of papers he retained, including magazine articles, newspaper clippings, letters, speeches, and upon interviews with Boerner's friends, relatives and business associates. His research records and working papers are now in the archives at Cornell University. Since new roses are introduced each year and Boerner's contribution to that field does not depend upon last year's market or last year's awards, no effort has been made to update the appendix of his patented roses which refers to honors awarded Boerner's roses through 1971.

Wells is the author of sixteen previously-published books as well as several hundred short stories and articles for national magazines. His books have won awards from the Wisconsin State Historical Society, the Milwaukee County Historical Society, the Council for Wisconsin Writers and the Boys' Club of America. Seven of his short stories have appeared in anthologies, several have been adapted for television or radio and many have been reprinted abroad.

Wells retired in 1984 from the editorial staff of *The Milwaukee Journal,* where he had worked since leaving the World War II Navy in 1946. He and his wife, Edith, are now residents of Bisbee, Arizona, but spend their summers in Wisconsin, where two of their four grown children live.

We owe our special thanks to Professor Ralph M. Aderman, who has reviewed, edited and prepared the manuscript for printing; to JoAnna Poehlmann, who designed the jacket and aided in the design of the book; to Darlene Waterstreet, who prepared the two indexes; and to Mae Cooper Lunay, who was Boerner's trusted assistant at Jackson & Perkins and was an invaluable aid in organizing the papers he left at his death.

R. L. B.

Papa Floribunda

Chapter 1

A Rose In His Hat

"To presume to have made a masterpiece is just a little
beyond the realm of reality. But to be aiming toward the
dream rose is the incentive...." — Eugene S. Boerner.

The Cadillac nosed out of the driveway at Gene's Landing before the
sun was up and sped through the sleeping countryside toward the
northern New York community of Newark. Gene Boerner drove like a
man in a hurry, and he was. "I want to get there while the dew is still on
my roses," he would have had to explain if a policeman pulled alongside
to inquire why his right foot was so heavy. That would have been the
simple truth, although it was not the sort of excuse likely to appeal to a
cop at 6 a.m.

Boerner knew every inch of the thirty miles between his house on
Seneca Lake and the Jackson & Perkins nursery in Newark, for these
early morning drives were routine. When a man is in the business of
creating roses, he must make his rounds early. Before most Newark
residents had finished their morning coffee, he expected to have looked
at hundreds of his rose seedlings, judging them, deciding their fate. It
was better to do this while they were fresh as the dawn.

While he drove, numbers followed themselves through his head —
coded designations of recent crosses he had made between carefully
chosen rose parents. Over a year's time he might make ten thousand
such crosses — doing the job himself or, more likely, issuing orders
about which rose's pollen should be dusted on which other rose. Of those
ten thousand experiments in hybridization, perhaps four or five would
turn out to be worth keeping.

Charlie Perkins, president of the firm that had become the world's largest growers of roses, often joined him on such early morning walks through the rose fields. But today he had an appointment to meet one of those garden editors who came in an intermittent procession to talk to the man who had fathered more new roses than anyone else in history. Boerner welcomed such visits, viewing them as good promotion. He was one part artist and one part scientist, but he was also one part business-man who recognized that once a rose had been developed it should be sold at a profit. Besides, such interviews gave him someone new to talk to, and Boerner was a man who liked to talk, particularly if the talk was about roses.

He parked his car and walked rapidly toward the test fields. The editor was waiting. Gene stopped and picked a yellow rose for the man's lapel. He already had pinned a red rose to his own jacket, plucked from one of the flower beds at Gene's Landing, the venerable cobblestone house where he lived.

"We'll talk while I make my rounds," he told the visitor, starting down the path.

"I see you have a notebook. That's to keep track of how the roses are doing, I suppose?"

"That's right. Sometimes I use a tape recorder instead and just talk into it. In any case, I want to get my impressions down while they're fresh."

"Exactly what are you looking for?"

"Many things. The plant's health and vigor. The beauty of the bud as well as the blossom. The fragrance."

He bent over and peered at a white rose, then picked it, and put it under his hat, walking on down the rows of bushes as though nothing had happened.

"Why'd you do that?" the visitor asked.

Gene laughed. "It's an old habit of mine. I let the rose ride along up there, then take it out and check its fragrance. The aroma is stronger after the blossom has been warmed for a while. Fragrance is important to me. It's one of the unpredictable things about crossing roses; you're never sure ahead of time how it's going to turn out. There are some fine roses that have little or no aroma, but they'd be better if they smelled pretty. They ought to smell like roses."

"What about colors? I suppose you're breeding for new shades."

"Yes. I want a rose that's different enough from the established varieties so a gardener will be interested in adding it to his collection. The colors must be distinctive, clear and appealing to the eye. When the colors fade, they should do so gracefully, not turn some dingy shade after the bloom is past its peak."

"For example?"

"Well, take Pinocchio. Its blooms go through several color changes before dying away completely, all the changes pleasant to look at. Other points I look for are a maximum of flowers, a minimum of thorns, strong stems, disease resistance, self-cleaning ability, and — "

"Self-cleaning ability?"

"That means the petals should drop off when they become wilted instead of staying on and spoiling the effect of the other blossoms."

The men walked on for a while, Boerner peering this way and that at the beds of rose bushes that were being tested to see whether they would be worth patenting and adding to the list of those available in the J. & P. catalogue that went to two million potential customers each winter, giving them something to dream about while the weather was too cold to dig in the ground. If all went well, many of these gardeners would convert their dreams into orders for Jackson & Perkins' roses.

"Katharine Kinkead did a fine piece about you and your roses in *The New Yorker*," the visitor observed. "I liked what she said about roses having come a long way in a short time and how you were one of those who could congratulate themselves for having done a great deal to bring the rose to its present high estate."

Boerner fumbled in his pocket. He brought forth a worn copy of the magazine article. "Here's a quotation I liked," he said. "It says, 'While the rose is only one of a great many things that have changed spectacularly over the last third of a century, it is one of the very few that have changed spectacularly for the better.' Now there's a statement I agree with, one hundred per cent!"

When the garden editor had enough notes to satisfy him and was preparing to leave, Boerner insisted that he take along a bouquet of roses for his wife. It was more than just a friendly gesture. It was a way of giving the visitor a chance to look at the blossoms at his leisure and absorb their beauty.

At this stage in Eugene Boerner's career it was natural for anyone who planned to write an article about roses to make a pilgrimage to Newark to talk with him. Since he had arrived there in 1920 to join the nursery, it had grown into the world's largest producer of roses and as its chief hybridist he had become internationally known. By now J. & P. was doing an annual business of more than ten million dollars, with roses responsible for three-fourths of that total. Around Newark the rose was not only a thing of beauty but big business — a highly competitive one, too, using sophisticated promotional techniques to sustain a mass market for its product. As Miss Kinkead had observed, the changes in both the flower and in the methods of bringing it to market had been both rapid and profound. It was more difficult to build obsolescence into a rose than an automobile, but nurserymen came out with annual model changes, just like Detroit. Prior to each new growing season, Jackson & Perkins and its rivals tried to find new varieties which hundreds of thousands of gardeners could be persuaded they couldn't quite live without.

The best way to create such a demand was to patent a rose which could be pointed to as a winner in the competition sponsored by the nurserymen's trade association, All-America Rose Selections, Inc. — more commonly called AARS. This honor had commercial connotations, but it was not achieved lightly. A rose chosen as one of the annual AARS winners had to run the gauntlet of some of the nation's hardest-to-please growers. Often only one or two new roses scored high enough in a twelve-month period to qualify for the honor, which could be compared to a Hollywood Oscar except that it was less subject to behind-the-scenes politicking than the movie capital's promotional contest.

The firm of which Boerner was part owner sold more roses than anyone else, but it accounted for only a small percentage of the seventy-five million rose bushes sold annually in the United States for a gross of perhaps $200,000,000 at this period in the nineteen-fifties. Americans were by no means history's most enthusiastic rose nuts, however. That distinction belongs to the ancient Romans, some of whom slept on transparent mattresses filled with rose petals, took their ease next to fountains spraying rose water, ate rose pudding, drank rose wine, and then, to combat their rosy hangovers, downed rose tonic the morning after.

Still, the flower's popularity in the fifties was so well entrenched on both sides of the Atlantic that the holder of a patent on a particularly-admired variety might receive as much as half a million dollars in royalties during the seventeen years his creation was protected. As the most prolific of such creators of new roses, Boerner had assigned the royalties to his company, so did not profit from them directly. By now, in fact, his roses' royalties were one of the firm's major assets.

With the bulk of the company's business now in the mail-order field, it was necessary to bring out new roses each year to keep gardeners interested. Each new spring catalogue included perhaps ten new roses, most of them Boerner's. The firm also competed for the right to introduce especially-promising creations of other American and European hybridists. J. & P. made arrangements with some of its competitors to grow and market their best roses, paying as much as $300,000 a year for the privilege. The competitors, in turn, paid Jackson & Perkins for the right to market Boerner's roses.

Each new rose created by Boerner for the company represented seven or more years of work and an investment of $50,000 in research. Whether J. & P. would get back its investment from any particular rose was always a gamble. In the case of a hybrid picked as an All-America Rose Selection, however, the prospects were nearly certain. Charles Perkins estimated that an AARS award meant a minimum sale of one hundred fifty thousand bushes for the firm the first year, with brisk demand continuing for years to come.

During his career, Boerner fathered fourteen such AARS winners, all but three of them floribundas — a type of rose few Americans had heard of until he rescued cuttings from Germany just ahead of World War II and began to concentrate much of his formidable energies on improving and promoting it. By the mid-fifties one national magazine reported that "almost singlehandedly," Gene Boerner has made the floribunda so popular that it is crowding the long-established hybrid tea for top selling honors. And another magazine article noted that "perhaps no other flowering shrub in the past twenty-five years has inspired more enthusiasm among gardeners.... All over America, whenever roses are planted in gardens, the floribunda is literally taking over."

By this period of his long career, three out of each four patented rose bushes being sold were floribundas. Between 1944 and 1954 floribunda sales increased by no less than fifteen hundred percent. Such remarkable success had given Boerner a nickname, "Papa Floribunda." He looked that part — jovial, well-fed, hearty, an outgoing sort of fellow with brown eyes, a ruddy face set off by a luxuriant mustache, a booming voice, and the kind of enthusiasm for his life's work that was downright infectious.

Roses were not only his occupation and his hobby, but, as a lifelong bachelor, he looked on them almost as part of his family. He joked about them being his children — "at least they don't talk back to their papa" —

but the remark was not entirely in jest. When one of his roses brought beauty to thousands of gardens and, not incidentally, profit to the company, he was as proud of its success as a father whose son or daughter has just made Phi Beta Kappa.

Chapter II

Setting Down Roots

History's most prolific rose hybridizer was a grandson of a Wisconsin pioneer. The grandfather's decision to move to that cold climate had a direct bearing on Gene Boerner's attitude toward the development of the rose. Hence, it had an indirect bearing on the varieties being grown in tens of thousands of gardens in America and Europe in the 1970s. No one who grew up in Cedarburg, Wisconsin, would be likely to forget what can happen to a rose bush in a northern winter. When Gene was a boy around the turn of the century, the selection available to northern rose fanciers was limited. When he had a chance to do something about this by developing new strains, the memory of subzero winters of his youth prompted him to insist that the improved varieties must be hardy as well as beautiful. An ability to survive without coddling was one of the principal advantages he admired in the floribunda.

The reason Gene was born in Cedarburg on January 22, 1893 was that his grandpa, a native of Hatten, Germany, had decided to settle there more than fifty years before. After migrating to the United States in 1837, Christoph Friedrich Börner, who anglicized the name to C. Frederick Boerner, was one of many young Europeans who saw a more attractive future open to them in America. He opened a general store in Charleston, South Carolina, where his sister and her husband were living. He prospered to the point where he added a second store within a few years.

By 1846, however, he was becoming restless again. There was talk of the opportunities to be found on the western frontier, and many of the more vigorous young men along the Eastern seaboard were heading in that direction. Frederick Boerner joined them, setting out on a prospecting visit to what was then called Wisconsin Territory, a region that was on the eve of a vast influx of migrants from Europe. The newcomers came mostly from Boerner's native land. They would soon make Milwaukee and some smaller Wisconsin cities seem for a time like German rather than American communities.

The rail link between Chicago and Milwaukee would not be completed for another nine years, so Frederick must have arrived either by stagecoach or Great Lakes ship. He found Milwaukee a rough, brawling boom town of raw new buildings and soaring hopes. It was growing rapidly, its agents meeting passenger ships in New York and trying to convince the arriving immigrants that if they were so foolish as to settle in Chicago, then a city of about thirty thousand residents, they would catch the cholera.

C. Friedrich Börner, originally from Hatten, Germany, the grandfather of Eugene S. Boerner.

Boerner was not impressed with Milwaukee as a future home, but he liked the region a few miles farther north. In 1846 he visited Cedarburg, where two South Carolina friends who had borrowed money from him had selected the site and laid out the town. Taken with the wooded area, now a bedroom community for commuters from Milwaukee, he decided to settle there with his family. In 1848, the year Wisconsin became a state, he made a trip back home to Oldenburg, Germany, to enlist further recruits for the Wisconsin colony.

This was a time of troubles in Europe, with revolutionary movements organized to overthrow or at least lessen the authority of monarchial rule. When the movements failed, many Germans left for America, often heading directly toward the cheap land available on the Wisconsin frontier. In that vicinity these "Forty-Eighters" became a Germanic equivalent of the Pilgrim fathers of early New England.

In Charleston, Boerner had married another German immigrant, Helena Hussmann. By the time they moved to Cedarburg in 1849, they were the parents of a son, named for his father. Five other children were born to them. But life was an uncertain matter on the frontier, particularly for the young. Life expectancy at birth was then less than eighteen years in Wisconsin. Epidemics were common. Medical care was primitive. So five of the six children of Frederick and Helena Boerner died young, three of them within a six-week period in 1862 during a diptheria outbreak. Arthur R. Boerner, the youngest, was the only one of Helena Boerner's children to survive to maturity.

When he was less than a year old, his mother died. In her letters that have survived there were frequent references to flower seeds and plants, so it is obvious that, like most pioneer women, she was interested in the practicalities of dooryard horticulture. According to family tradition, a children's playground and an arbor on the farm which she and her husband bought in Cedarburg were planned and planted by her, so her life had an indirect bearing on that of her grandson, Eugene, across the long years that separated them.

With a baby in the house, Frederick Boerner waited only three months to take a second wife. He chose seventeen-year-old Anna Vosteen, a distant cousin, and, like him, a native of Hatten. Between 1860 and 1877, they became the parents of six sons and three daughters. Two of these nine children died before their sixth birthdays, but the others survived to share the big house with the surviving son of the first marriage.

The farm which C. Frederick bought in Cedarburg was a mile and a quarter long and a quarter of a mile wide, totaling two hundred acres. A pleasant stream, Cedar Creek, ran through its entire length. When the Boerners arrived, in 1849, part of the land had already been cleared. The first building put up was a barn, erected on the northern side of the property near a spring which provided water for the livestock. Then a house and another barn were built on the southerly portion of the two hundred acres. The house was an oblong shaped dwelling, one story plus a loft, with two rooms on each side of a central hall. Soon there was a one-story addition on the back and a porch on the front.

Two of Boerner's friends, William Schroeder and Frederick Hilgen, had arrived in Cedarburg before he did and had purchased the farm for him. He paid a total of $1,295 for the five forty-acre tracts, a little less than $6.50 an acre. Like other new settlers in a region largely covered by woods, he spent much of his time in the early years cutting down trees, using some of the wood for buildings and burning the rest to be rid of it. But he planted trees, too, most notably a spruce which was to rise majestically over the house when his grandchildren were young. He put in a cedar hedge. He or his wife planted a garden and a start was made on an orchard.

The orchard still bore fruit when his grandchildren were young, and some of the trees survived into the 1970s in altered form. A grandson, Arthur Boerner, saved some of the old varieties by grafting them onto his apple trees at his home in Brookfield, another Milwaukee suburb. Frederick obtained the seedlings from a nursery, Ellwanger & Barry, at twenty-five cents each, first going through the catalogue by the light of an oil lamp and checking off the varieties he wanted — Early Harvest, Early Joe, Holland Pippin, Summer Queen, Autumn Strawberry, Fall Pippin, Maiden's Blush, St. Lawrence, Baldwin, Yellow Bellflower, Fameuse, Northern Spy, Newtown Pippin, Rhode Island Greening, Russet Golden, Tetofsky, Esopus Spitzenberg and Seek-no-further. Yellow Bellflower was a particular favorite. Long after Frederick's death his grandsons looked forward to their ripening with impatience and, when the day came, ate them, in Arthur's words, "by the peck."

Frederick Boerner's first crop of wheat was raised in a field still filled with stumps and was threshed with flails on the barn floor. The grain was sowed by hand, with Boerner walking methodically back and forth across the field, dodging stumps, holding a panful of seed in his left hand, scattering it with his right. One of his children, Theodore, later recalled trying to help with this chore as a small boy and being told exactly how to go about it so "dass der Wind es nicht fort blaset" — that the wind does not blow it away.

Deer were plentiful. Passenger pigeons descended in great clouds. The larder was often replenished with a rifle or shotgun. Fish were numerous in the unpolluted streams. The winters were cold, but the growing season was long enough and the soil rich enough to make farming profitable. However, Boerner was not content to live solely off the land. From the beginning he was an investor and businessman as well as a farmer, having brought some capital with him from Charleston.

Seven years after he arrived in Cedarburg he began selling off parts of his farm. During the next six years he sold all but about fifty-five acres at prices ranging from $25 to $50 an acre so that he realized more than double his original investment while retaining the portion containing the house, barn, orchard, and a twelve-acre woods he had left standing from the original forest. Because of a peculiarity of the original deed, his residual holdings included about ten acres that were underwater; a third of a mile of Cedar Creek was contained within the farm's boundaries.

In the early 1850s Boerner put up a three-story brick building at the corner of Oneida (now East Wells) and Market Streets in Milwaukee, the present location of the Marshall and Ilsley Bank. He had trouble collecting rent from his tenants there, so he moved his family into the

Cedarburg's streets were congested with farmers' horses and wagons on cattle fair day.

top floor and presumably operated a store on the ground floor. By 1864, however, he was back at the farm in Cedarburg. Shortly afterward he traded his Milwaukee building to his brother, Christian, for a store which the latter had opened in Cedarburg.

The Cedarburg property extended from Washington Street to what was then Velvet Street, now more prosaically called Third. Next door was the Washington House, a rambling frame structure. The grounds widened behind the Boerner store into a large field, used as a pasture for cows and horses, with a brook running across it. The combination store and residence had a large side yard, separated from the garden by a picket fence, with room for a wagon shed and other outbuildings. A wide wooden porch with an ornamental railing extended along the residence half of the main building. The parlor with its horsehair furniture and bouquets of wax flowers was on the first floor, as were the kitchen and dining room. Most of the family's time was spent on the second floor in a room above the parlor, the children studying their lessons or playing, the parents talking or reading, with the conversation generally in the ancestral German.

The Turn Verein movement was at its height among German-Americans, and Boerner joined the Cedarburg branch, which was the center of the community's social life. Arthur, the oldest boy, and his brothers took part in the gymnastics at the Turn Verein Hall under the instruction of Henry Wehausen and practiced on a turning pole and trapeze which their father put up near the barn.

By 1860 Cedarburg had two general stores, a hotel, two meat markets, a grist mill, and an apothecary shop. It was connected with Milwaukee by stagecoach. There were two resident physicians. Once a month, on what was called Fair Day, a dentist arrived to take care of any toothaches that had developed during the last thirty days. The custom of a monthly Fair Day continued in Cedarburg for a half century or more. Nearby farmers rose at dawn to hitch up their horses and haul produce to the village, competing for the best parking places. Cattle and swine were driven into the little town to be sold. Boerner and the other local merchants ordered special merchandise for the occasion and tried to lure the crowds of shoppers into their stores. Small boys darted in and out. Women in long dresses strolled about or haggled with the salesmen. The men exchanged news, traded horses, talked politics and, in general, took advantage of this holiday from the regular routine.

Within a few years after Eugene Boerner's grandfather began operating his Cedarburg store, the Cedarburg Woolen Mill opened, encouraging the town to grow. Wooden sidewalks replaced the gravel or mud walks. Soon the village even had street lights — kerosene lamps hung on posts. Each morning the lamplighter pulled a child's wagon laden with lamps along the streets, stopping at each pole to trade a filled lamp for an empty one. Each evening he returned to light them at dusk, unless there promised to be a bright moon. In that case, the lamps were not considered necessary.

Employees and customers of the Boerner Brothers store line up on the sidewalk to have their picture taken (1906).

Residents had a choice of two Lutheran churches and a Roman Catholic church; two more Lutheran churches were added later, along with one for the Methodists. By 1866 a branch of the Second Ward Savings Bank of Milwaukee was opened. The Second Ward was known as the brewers' bank, with members of Milwaukee's rising aristocracy of beer running its affairs. Not long after the branch opened, a rumor spread through Cedarburg that it was in trouble. Depositors gathered in a worried group at the door and demanded their money. So many showed up that there wasn't enough cash available to satisfy them. A messenger on a fast horse galloped to Milwaukee to inform the home office, and soon an express wagon with money to pay the clamoring farmers and villagers arrived. The bank had been sound enough (in Milwaukee, at least, it was understood that beer was a perfectly sound foundation for finance), and many of those who had been most anxious to take their money out soon returned sheepishly and put it back again. But the brewers were offended. The branch soon closed. It was not until 1893 that Cedarburg had a banking institution again.

Like many other settlers, Boerner was asked to invest money to ensure that a railroad would be routed near his place of business. As happened with monotonous regularity in the early days of Wisconsin railroading, the line he invested in went bankrupt and he lost his bonds. By 1870, however, the Milwaukee & Northern was chartered and built a line through Cedarburg. The arrival of this predecessor of the Milwaukee Road was greeted with enthusiasm. A banquet was held at the Turner Hall, with railway officials and local civic leaders congratulating each other. Boerner was glad enough to see the railroad, but his earlier experience with the bankrupt line had soured him on this method of transportation, and he usually preferred to use his horse and wagon instead of riding the train to Milwaukee.

Such a trip took all day, with the wagon loaded with apples, eggs, butter, and other produce to be sold in the city. Several of his children often went along. Toward evening the wagon would head north again filled with merchandise for the store, the youngsters fighting to stay awake, the father leaning back in the driver's seat and singing songs he remembered from his boyhood in Germany.

In 1876, Boerner treated himself to a trip to the Centennial Exposition in Philadelphia, coming home with stories of "das wunderbare Licht," the electric light which was first shown to the public there. That was also the year when the oldest son, Arthur, left home. He spent six months at Spencerian Business College in Milwaukee, then looked for a job in that city.

"In the beginning, you must not ask about wages," his father advised him. "First you must show the people what you can accomplish."

The eighteen-year-old landed a job as a shipping clerk with Ed Ascherman & Co., which bragged it was the largest wholesale cigar-maker in the Northwest. His father continued to send him suggestions on how to get ahead: "Do nothing that can injure your good name. Do not go into bad company." The elder Boerner also asked Arthur to keep an eye on his younger brother Gustave, who was now enrolled in the business college.

In September of 1878, C. Frederick Boerner died, aged sixty-six. At once, the life of his oldest son changed drastically. Instead of being a boy trying to find a modest place for himself on the lower rungs of the business ladder, Arthur at the age of twenty was faced with being the male head of a large family. Except for Gustave, his five half-brothers and two half-sisters were still too young to be of much help. His stepmother, Anna, was not a businesswoman. There was the store to look after, the farm to oversee. Arthur had plans and ambitions of his own, including the first stirrings of a plan to give up commerce for a career in medicine. But his new status left him little choice. He went home to Cedarburg to take on his new responsibilities.

Chapter III

Boyhood In A Country Town

After C. Frederick's death the family business became Boerner Brothers, with the two oldest sons acting as partners and several of the other boys joining the firm as they got old enough. The store prospered. Still, Arthur was not sure he wanted to spend the rest of his life selling merchandise in a small town. Four years after his father's death, when it seemed that his younger brothers could handle the family business, he went to New York and enrolled in Bellevue Hospital Medical College.

What a change that must have been for a twenty-four-year-old who had never been farther from Cedarburg than Milwaukee and who was used to the easygoing routine of a hometown where to be a Boerner was to be a leading citizen. But there was some of the restless spirit in Arthur that had been in his father when C. Frederick was young. The transition from Germany to Charleston and then to the Wisconsin frontier could have been no more striking than the contrast between Cedarburg and Manhattan in 1882.

The break was a temporary one. While Arthur was at Bellevue, the store did not do well without him, so he returned home, abandoning his plans for a medical career. Seven years later he tried to break away again, not as complete a change this time nor as long a journey, but one last attempt to get out from under the primary responsibility for the Cedarburg store his father had left him. He went to work for the Heyn Department Store on East Wisconsin Avenue in Milwaukee, heading one of its departments. He continued to have an interest in Boerner Brothers, however, and after two years he went back to Cedarburg to help the family company expand into an early version of a chain store operation. Boerner Brothers opened a branch at Saukville, Wisconsin, with a younger brother, Henry, in charge, later moving this store's operations to the larger community of Port Washington. A third store was opened in West Bend. Oscar Boerner ran this one.

Meanwhile, Arthur had met Hermine Sonnenberg, the daughter of a Frankfurt alderman, who had arrived from Germany to visit friends in Milwaukee. They were married February 25, 1886. Thirteen months

Hermine Sonnenberg, who married Arthur Boerner on February 25, 1886. She was the mother of ten children, nine of whom were boys.

later, their first son was born and named for his father. Having sons became something of a habit. Ten children were born, all but two of whom lived to maturity, and nine of them were boys. The single exception was Helene. She was younger than Arthur, Herman, and William and two years older than the fifth child, Eugene Sonnenberg Boerner, who arrived on January 22, 1893. Another son, George, was born the following year but lived only sixteen days. Then came a six-year gap in the family birth statistics before Robert was born in 1899, followed by Alfred in 1900, Walter (who died as a baby) in 1902 and Carl, the last, in 1905. So, although Eugene was technically a middle child, the fifth of ten children, he spent the formative years before his seventh birthday as the youngest member of his family.

It was a large and closely knit clan, with aunts and uncles and cousins nearby and Grandma Anna, now affectionately called Oma, on the old farm with the cedar hedge. Being for a time the youngest son of the oldest son had its advantages. Eugene lost that status when Robert was born, but by then he was firmly enthroned as the favorite, particularly with his grandmother, his unmarried Aunt Ida, and his Uncle Albert, a Boerner who did not take happily to the family business and whose decision to operate a plant nursery on a portion of the family farm had a considerable influence on Gene's career as the nation's leading rose hybridist.

Eugene's habit of European travel, which was characteristic of his later life, began when he was a year old. In 1894, with the family firm prospering, the parents and five children went to Germany so Mrs. Boerner's parents could see their grandchildren for the first time. The daughter, who became Mrs. Helene Schlueter, was only three years old at the time, but she still remembered how Eugene yelled his displeasure when the foghorn sounded as they boarded the ship in New York.

Mrs. Boerner and the five children, along with her sister and a maid, set up housekeeping in a pension near her parents' home in Frankfurt. Her husband spent part of the year-long visit in Italy. He felt the sun would be good for his health, which was less than robust. While they were apart, the Boerners wrote each other every day. The wife's letters were full of the doings of her lively family, including accounts of the conquest that the baby, Eugene, had made of his European relatives.

When the long vacation was over and the family was back in Cedarburg, Arthur Boerner, Sr., plunged with new vigor into the business of getting ahead. With his brothers he formed an investment company, and they put their surplus funds into a variety of enterprises ranging from neighborhood creameries, shoe and furniture factories to a northern iron mine rich in manganese. The Boerner Brothers Company also invested in the Gilson Foundry and Machine Shop (later Gilson Manufacturing Company) in Port Washington at a time when it had only a dozen employees. The foundry and machine works soon grew and branched out to become a builder of gasoline engines at a time when such engines were rapidly replacing the horse. The 1890s were a period when the United States was changing from an agricultural to an industrial economy. Some Americans were getting rich in the process, and a lot of others, including the Boerners, were trying to get their share of what was called McKinley prosperity.

Eugene was too young to be concerned with such things, but his life was full enough without having to worry about the price of manganese. The family lived in a fine, big house in the village. In 1899, when the boy was six years old, Arthur Boerner astonished the neighbors by installing what he called his "waterworks," which not only provided running water for the kitchen but made the Boerner house the only one in Cedarburg which did not need a backyard privy. The family could afford a hired girl, who was paid $3.00 a week and board, and a *kindermädchen* who took care of the children for $1.50 a week and keep. With three older brothers and a sister as well as an excellent supply of cousins, Eugene found the household a lively and challenging one, full of talk and laughter, good food, and warmth.

Cedar Creek was dammed near the Boerner house, forming a pond where boys and girls and some of the adults skated back and forth or around and about during the long Wisconsin winters. When the ice melted, it was a handy place to fish. Eugene got his name in the paper and won the envious admiration of every boy in town when he caught a record-sized carp at an age when he was hardly big enough to carry it home.

Another fortunate aspect about the neighborhood from a small boy's viewpoint was the nearness of the village firehouse. When the firebell clanged to summon the volunteer firemen, Gene dashed down the street with the other boys to find out what was burning. Between such exciting occasions there was the chance to watch the amateur fireman preparing themselves for the next emergency by filling the tank of the horsedrawn engine at the creek across the street from the Boerner house.

Cedarburg was still a small and relatively isolated village, but it was plentifully supplied with churches. Following a custom begun in the Middle Ages in Germany, their bells were rung each Saturday night. In the old days there had been a reason for this: The unfriendly spirits must be chased out of town before the Sabbath. In the wise and advanced times around the turn of the century, hardly anyone believed that the bells were still needed to frighten off the ghosts, but the Saturday night clangor had been customary in the Fatherland so it was continued in those Wisconsin communities, like Cedarburg, where German settlers predominated.

The Boerners attended Immanuel Lutheran Church at first, later switching their allegiance to the Church of the Advent Lutherans. But Trinity Lutheran was across the street from their house, and it was there that Gene made friends with the janitor. When it was nearly time for the bells to ring, the boy would dash across the road — trying to remember to look both ways for horses and buggies — and hang around in the hope that he would be allowed to help with the ringing.

The great rope dangled from the dusty belfry, ready to be pulled. The janitor could do the job while keeping both feet on the floor; but when Gene was allowed to ring the Saturday bell, he had to swing up and down, feeling the tug and pull and shudder of the iron-voiced noise-maker above him. How glorious it was to know that the clamor he was making could be heard all over town, know, too, that there wasn't a boy within earshot who wouldn't have traded his favorite pocket knife to take his place.

The church bells ring any old way on Saturday nights, so it didn't matter whether the rope was pulled by an adult or the weight of a small boy. The Saturday bells were festive, even though their sound was the signal for a solemn weekly ceremony — the wooden tubs placed in every kitchen, the water heated on the rectangular cast-iron cookstoves, then the family members in a rigidly established order of precedence taking turns at the Saturday night baths.

The church bells also rang on Sunday mornings, of course. But dignity was required then, so the janitor did the job himself. They rang for funerals, but Gene's ambition did not extend to handling that duty. When a member of the congregation died, the bell must toll slowly as befitted the occasion, ringing once for each year of the departed's age, then pausing for breath, tolling the years once more, pausing again before tolling a third and final time. When the solemn knell began, everyone stopped what he was doing and began counting. By adding up the number it was generally possible to decide which resident of the little town was being buried that day. In the case of women who had been trying to keep their birthdays secret, the bell announced for all to hear the truth that she had hidden in her lifetime.

Feeling the soft strength of the rope in his hands on those Saturday nights was only one of the joys open to the boy, although it ranked high on his list. Riding Whiskers, the family pony, or being pulled in the bouncing two-wheeled cart as the Shetland trotted along was equally exciting. The way Whiskers joined the household is an indication of how much trouble Gene's parents sometimes took to make life fun for their children. During the Christmas season when Eugene was four or five years old, the family was going about its business when there was a sudden blast on a bugle from outside the house. Everyone made a dash for the door. Standing there in the snow was Santa Claus, the bugle in one hand, the pony's reins in the other. Not until several years later did Gene decide that the jolly fellow in the red suit and white whiskers had merely been the hired man.

The pony made it easier for him to visit his grandmother's farm, where Aunt Ida and Grandma Oma welcomed him with affection reinforced with an endless supply of cookies. If it was spring or summer, he would stop along the way to pick wildflowers. Oma would already have a bouquet on the kitchen table, but she could always find a place for more. She especially admired the white violets Eugene sometimes found; they were scarce even then, so particularly valuable. As he grew older, she encouraged him to pick the garden flowers and arrange them with some attention to artistic balance. There is no reason to suppose that she suspected the boy's future lay in horticulture. It was enough for her to share her liking for the beauty that springs from the earth and to be glad that she and her grandson had this in common.

When Gene grew old enough to help with the farm chores, he was assigned the task of milking the one cow that was kept by Oma to supply the larder. One of his early letters to Santa Claus had been preserved in which, along with toys, he requested a cow of his own. But this request doubtless came before he learned to milk. During the summers he spent at the farm, he came to hate the duty of going night and morning to the barn. He would have a farm when he grew up, he once told his sister, but it would have not a single dairy cow, a prediction that came true in both respects.

As Gene grew older, he also made himself useful at his Uncle Albert's nursery. The uncle had first tried his hand at storekeeping. He had been sent to West Bend to help his brother, Oscar, who was considered too easygoing. The traveling salesmen had a saying among themselves: "Anyone who can't sell Oscar Boerner can't sell anybody anything." With Albert planning to get married, a family council decided, he could lend Oscar a hand.

His fiancée, Emma, went to West Bend to prepare to set up housekeeping. She stayed at a rooming house where Ida, Arthur, and Herman Boerner were living. Emma and Albert were married on a Wednesday and left on their honeymoon. The following Saturday, she went back to her parents' house in Cedarburg to pick up the rest of her belongings. But she was too ill to go back to West Bend. The doctor was called. The diagnosis was typhoid fever.

The two Boerner sons and their aunt who had lived in the West Bend rooming house also contracted typhoid. They recovered but Albert's bride did not. After Emma's death he became a recluse, avoiding his friends and family. When he was finally able to return to work at the West Bend store, he was so obviously unhappy there that his brother Arthur suggested he try another way of making a living.

"If you don't like the business," he said, "why don't you start a nursery?"

And so the first plant nursery in Cedarburg was begun on a portion of the family farm. Running it was an occupation that suited Gene's Uncle Albert better. The time came when he married again; and, as his favorite nephew grew older, the nursery gave the youth his first taste of the satisfactions and hard work and disappointments and triumphs that come to those who earn a living by encouraging plants to grow.

Work was a part of every boy's lot in that time and place, but there was also leisure for fun. Amusement did not come packaged. There was

Gene Boerner lived with his brothers and sister in the large comfortable house in Cedarburg.

no radio, no movies, no television. There were so few modern advantages, in fact, that there was time to walk in the fields and woods, to skate on the frozen creek in winter, to fish and swim there in summer. The virgin woods Gene's grandfather had left as an example of the original forest was a favorite refuge of the Boerner boys. There were portions of untouched prairieland in the vicinity, too. The farm provided a kind of open air laboratory for a youth who was interested in things that grew. It is unlikely that Gene or his brothers regarded it in quite that light, but they roamed widely and freely, in common with small town boys of their time, keeping lists of birds they had seen, noticing what growing conditions were most favorable for wild orchids or any of a hundred other species that were part of their inheritance. In the Boerner yard were apple, plum, and peach trees, but the cherry tree that hung its bounty over the sidewalk was the boys' particular favorite. With the others, Gene would sit on a branch and eat the fruit, saving the cherry pits to fling at unwary passersby.

Special days arrived regularly throughout the year. Gene's father's birthday on January 26, for example, was an annual excuse for a champagne party. His friends and relatives gathered to toast him, then settled down to play a serious game of skat, the children keeping quiet in order to be allowed to watch. Other birthdays — there were plenty of them in this large family with its numerous aunts and uncles and cousins — called for less formal parties. Gene's was on January 22, his sister's on January 23, so when they were young they often had a combined celebration. The one in 1899 stood out in family memories.

The "waterworks" had just been installed. Thirty small boys and girls, none of whom had ever seen such a marvel before, kept dodging in and out of the tiny bathroom to inspect the modern wonder, a flush toilet. The dangling chain was pulled so often with so much enthusiasm that something went wrong with the mechanism. The bowl overflowed, the hired girl came running with mop and pail, and such a hubbub and commotion arose that the Boerner birthday party was the talk of the elementary school social leaders for months.

Every Sunday dinner was a special occasion when Gene was young. There was usually a leg of veal, lettuce with sour-cream dressing, such desserts as homemade ice cream or a chocolate pudding of a quality unknown in our time of prepared mixes that come in boxes — the recipe called for four eggs and whipped cream, among other things. After everyone was thoroughly stuffed, the hired man would hitch the horse to a canopy-topped buggy and the parents would drive to Grandma Oma's house, the children walking along behind. There would be uncles, aunts, and cousins there; and if the weather was pleasant, there might be a ball game or a tennis match on the first lawn tennis court in Cedarburg. In the evening another big meal was prepared, a kind of Teutonic smorgasbord with cold tongue, cold ham, cold veal, and whatever else the ingenuity of half a dozen hearty cooks had contrived. Each of the women brought food to the gathering and took pride in offering a dish that would pass muster with the resident critics. There was not the slightest likelihood of a child going to bed hungry after an afternoon at Grandma Oma's.

Food was important. The smells of cooking were a part of Gene's early life, the aromas permeating his childhood. On Saturdays, for instance, his mother often baked a dozen coffee cakes, going heavy on the butter and sugar. The bread was homemade, of course. Lentil soup was a favorite, flavored with bacon or ham and either vinegar or tomatoes, the blend striking the nostrils of a hungry boy as soon as he opened the front door.

The rest of the year's special occasions paled beside the traditions

Gene often visited Grandma Oma's (Anna Vosteen Boerner) at Cedar Hedge.

associated with Christmas. Preparations began as soon as the Thanksgiving feasting had ended. On December 6, St. Nicholas Day, it was time for Gene and the other children to hang their stockings from the bedposts. Each morning from then until Christmas they leaped out of bed to discover what had materialized in the sock overnight. They were never disappointed — well, hardly ever. One morning Helene found a bottle of cod liver oil in her stocking, which hardly seemed festive. Usually the gift was a lollipop, a penny, or some other small token. Occasionally it was that rare and exotic fruit, the orange, seldom seen then in Wisconsin except on special occasions.

Several days before Christmas the tree was brought into the parlor, a sheet was laid on the rug to catch drippings from the candles, and the room was declared out of bounds for those still young enough to believe in Santa. The older boys had the privilege of trimming the tree. The younger ones peered through the keyhole to watch. One year Herman prepared a small funnel out of rolled paper; and when Bob's eye appeared at the keyhole, he blew a fine cloud of flour into his brother's face. On Christmas, after the excitement of opening the presents had subsided, there was roast goose with apple-flavored stuffing and a choice of at least three kinds of pie.

The Boerners had one of the first automobiles in Cedarburg, an Oldsmobile. It was a two-seater in which the back of the front seat also served as the back of the rear seat so that those in front could see where they were going and those in back could see where they'd been. As the president of a company that was in the investment business as well as chain store merchandising, Arthur Boerner had to make frequent trips to such neighboring villages as Port Washington. Often a boy or two rode along for company on an auto trip that was anything but routine. The roads were hub deep in mud after a rain, dusty or rutted on other occasions, virtually impassable to anything but a horsedrawn sleigh in winter. The car, which was persuaded into life by spinning a crank, was likely to have a blowout or some other interesting ailment along the way. When the Olds met a horse that had not yet become philosophical about the encroachments of the machine age, it might be necessary to brake to a dead stop, with Boerner and his sons leaping out of the car to grab the animal's head and talk soothingly to it until it had calmed down.

Gene was a gregarious boy, constantly in motion. If he wasn't visiting the houses and, not incidentally, the larders of his relatives, he might go calling on the Kuethers, a neighboring family. Saturday night

Mrs. Kuether usually served sausages and egg pancakes, along with a variety of doughnuts called fried cakes, so Saturday night was the time Gene usually chose to call. He and the other boys were impressed by Kuether's bulk — he weighed in the neighborhood of three hundred pounds — and by his habit of cleaning his handlebar mustache by running a fork through it. Kuether was bald and wore a wig. In winter the Boerner boys liked to lay in ambush for him as he headed toward his job in the family store, then let fly with a barrage of snowballs. If Keuther's hat was knocked off, the skirmish was considered a success. If his wig came with it, it was a triumph.

On rainy days the attic was the place to go. It was full of the artifacts of a large and prosperous family which seldom threw anything away. By the time Gene was old enough to rummage through the magazines there, it contained no less than six baby buggies of various styles, some made of leather, some of reed, one with an umbrella.

The storekeeper was an avid reader, so his sons and daughter found great piles of old magazines in the attic. Besides *St. Nicholas* and *Youth's Companion,* bought for the children, there were copies of *Harper's* dating back to the Civil War. Gene read them eagerly, sometimes in the dusty attic, sometimes stretched full length under his favorite table downstairs. The attic was also a handy place to keep collections of rocks, old toys, dolls, tops, skates, and the kind of outdated clothing that can be used by children in unflattering imitations of their elder's abandoned fashions.

And so Gene's first thirteen years were spent in a family atmosphere that was secure, prosperous, settled, with enough discipline to maintain order and enough freedom to permit a boy to pursue his own interests. There was no reason for him to suppose that such conditions would not continue forever. But the period when his life would be safe and settled and certain was nearly over.

Chapter IV

The Easy Life Ends

There is a superstition among gamblers that luck moves in cycles, so that when the cards run well it is wise to bet heavily to build up a stake for the inevitable moment when everything will go wrong. The Boerners' luck had been good since eighteen-year-old Hermine Sonnenberg, the Frankfurt alderman's daughter, had married Arthur, the Cedarburg storekeeper. The family business was prospering, the children were strong and healthy, and in 1905 the future stretched out safe and serene. Mrs. Boerner was pregnant again — it would be, to no one's surprise, another boy — but after nine previous pregnancies there seemed no reason for concern about that. Mrs. Boerner was only thirty-eight years old, nine years younger than her husband, but somehow she felt old. She confided to the doctor that she tired more easily than she should. His diagnosis ended the family's safe and ordered routine. She had cancer. In 1905 such a pronouncement was a sentence of death.

When the family's luck turned, it turned with a vengeance. That September, while Mrs. Boerner was giving birth to a son, Carl — a child she knew she must soon leave — two of her other children were gravely ill with the typhoid fever contracted at the West Bend rooming house. Herman's case was relatively mild, but Arthur was so sick that there was worry over whether he would live. His father hired a male nurse, and gradually the eighteen-year-old Arthur and his seventeen-year-old brother got well again. But Art's plan to enroll at the University of Wisconsin that fall had to be postponed.

Twenty months later Mrs. Boerner died. During her lingering illness her husband's health also began to fail and his business fortunes to decline. It was hard to concentrate on investments or storekeeping while his more important future plans were falling apart. Among his losses was the manganese mine. He had bought on margin. If he could have hung onto the stock a little longer, the family always felt, he might have become rich. But he lost the $50,000 he had put into the speculation. Perhaps it no longer mattered very much to him just then whether he became rich or not.

The business reverses and his wife's death came almost simultane-
ously. He still had friends, however, and it was arranged that President
Theodore Roosevelt should appoint him postmaster. He did his duty by
the job and continued to serve as president of Boerner Brothers and to
take an interest in the family's other business activities, but the zest
had gone out of life for him.

As was natural for a boy whose playground had always been the
fields and woods, after his mother's death Gene turned for comfort to the
outdoors. He began to keep a diary with the inclusive title, "Notes on
Birds, Bugs, Beasts, and Flowers." In it he recorded a February 28, 1908
stroll to Poole's Swamp to look for the first robin. Robins are scarce in
Wisconsin in February. He saw none, but he found plenty of nuthatches,
crows, chickadees, and downy woodpeckers. On April 6, he noted,
spring's first hepatica was blooming by a brook. The diary entries
continued to record birds and beasts even after his father was left
partially paralyzed by a stroke early in 1909. But the entries ended in
the spring of that year as life became increasingly gloomy and uncertain
in the Boerner household.

Arthur Boerner, who had been head of the family since he was
twenty, died on June 7. At once, his oldest son — also named Arthur and
also in his twentieth year — found himself the head of the clan. As the
only girl among the eight orphaned children, sixteen-year-old Helene
helped keep house for her brothers, but an Austrian-born housekeeper,
Christine Pawlik, was hired, her duties including the care and dis-
ciplining of the younger Boerners. Arthur was working for the Gilson
Manufacturing Company in Port Washington and Herman and William
were old enough to be of some help in supporting the family, but the days
when the Boerners were regarded in Cedarburg as being among the
village's well-to-do were over. Eugene was sixteen when his father died.
Until then, it had never been necessary for him to worry much about
money because there had always been someone else to do the worrying.
But now, like his brothers and sister, he had to grow up and take his
share of responsibility.

With aunts, uncles, and a grandmother in the neighborhood, the
young Boerners were not entirely on their own. There were still those
calorie-laden suppers at Oma's, the parties on special occasions. Gene
continued to go to school as before, but in summer he got a job in a local
canning factory. It paid the relatively high wage of twenty-five cents an
hour. When the peas were ripe, it sometimes involved working eighteen

hours a day. He was able to put money aside for the day he'd be old enough for college.

In the summers Gene, his brothers, and sister lived in a tent camp on Cedar Hedge Farm called Thornapple Town.

During those summers the Boerner boys and their sister lived at what they called Thornapple Town, a camp next to the ten acres of woods their grandfather had left uncut on his farm to show future generations what the Wisconsin wilderness had been like when he first saw it. The boys built a shack which served as dining room and kitchen. They slept in tents with wooden floors. Helene cooked on an oil burner stove, rising early to pack a lunch for her brothers before they left for their jobs. Gene rode from the farm to the canning plant on his bicycle, pedaling sleepily through the silent town in the early morning, sometimes returning to the camp long after dark. Meanwhile, Helene, carrying water from nearby Cedar Creek, washed clothes by hand and took care of the other housekeeping chores.

Living there at the edge of the woods was primitive, but it was pleasant. In the spring the hawthorns were covered with pink and white blossoms. In the fall the red haws dangled from every branch. The creek was available for swimming. If a leech grabbed a toe, someone ran to the cook shack to get a handful of salt to pour on the bloodsucker so it would let go. When the weather was too cold for camping, it was necessary to move back under a more substantial roof; but the brothers and sister abandoned their gypsy life with regret.

Eugene was maturing fast, the process speeded by his father's death. There was less time for fun and boyish pranks now. There was need to look toward the future. Arthur encouraged him, although it was necessary to point out that money was no longer plentiful and if Gene planned to go to the university he must expect to work his way.

Gene had long talks with his older brother, who was scarcely more than a boy himself, with Arthur trying to take the place of the absent father and give the practical advice he felt was called for under the circumstances. The course of least resistance would be for Eugene to plan to go into the family store after high school or take advantage of the experience he'd had in helping Uncle Albert and join him in the nursery business. But Gene had other ideas. He wanted to be an engineer. Arthur told him that if his mind was made up, more power to him.

The days when Gene had had one of the finest soprano voices in the Lutheran choir were behind him. His voice had deepened to a robust bass. He was starting to take girls to parties and dances — nothing serious, everything casual and lighthearted as suited his age and the plan he had to leave Cedarburg for the life of a college boy. In a letter to Herman when Eugene was fifteen, he told of skating at the local rink and how the girls always grabbed for their skirts when they fell. "Miss Melvin's generally went up to the knees but they were quickly lowered," he reported. "It certainly was fun and I'm going again as soon as I can."

Albert, the youngest of his uncles, took a special interest in Gene after his father's death. A Spanish-American War veteran, a man whose comments could be abrupt and even cutting, Uncle Albert took some getting used to, but he and Gene got along splendidly most of the time. From trial and error Albert had accumulated a knowledge of how plants grow that made him a respected authority on the subject, and he passed along his store of practical information about horticulture to his nephew. As a method of promoting sales, Albert Boerner would work out landscaping plans for any client willing to put in shrubs and trees from the Cedar Hedge Farm Association. Gene went along on the landscaping jobs, helping dig the holes and plant the greenery.

Without knowing it, the boy was getting practical experience for what would become his life work, including the special skills needed for dealing with roses. The nursery's thirty-two-page catalogue included twenty-two kinds of hybrid perpetuals, three baby ramblers, fourteen "climbing, rambling and trailing roses," six moss roses, eleven shrub roses, and four of what were described as bedding roses. These last had to be lifted each fall and wintered in a cold frame.

Gene worked with his Uncle Albert at the nursery on Cedar Hedge Farm. A catalogue of its offerings is shown.

The varieties included Grüss an Teplitz, Madame Plantier, La France, Hermosa, Kaisern Augusta Victoria, Dorothy Perkins, Wichuraiana, and Harrison's Yellow. The Boerner nursery also offered such perennials as yarrow, coreopsis, fleabane, sneezewort, bergamot, and mullein. For a one-dollar fee, refundable with a three-dollar order, it offered "to show how your place can be laid out and planted in an effective way." Most of the roses cost 35 cents or $3.50 a dozen. The number of varieties listed indicated that even in Wisconsin's difficult winter climate customers were trying to grow some of the more delicate kinds. Some gardeners were apparently willing to dig them up each fall and protect them in a cold frame. It was obvious to anyone who dealt in roses in Wisconsin that a wider selection of hardy varieties would be useful.

The thought occurred to Gene as he went about with shovel and pruning shears, helping his uncle. The time would come when he would create roses especially for such climates. But that time was not yet. At the moment he was more concerned with school and such extra-curricular activities as his job as "sporting editor" of the high school yearbook, "The Orange and Black." He wrote a learned article about football for the issue of 1909, a year when one of the school songs was sung to a tune familiar to every Cedarburg boy, "Die Wacht am Rhein."

During his senior year Gene sat ahead of Erna Gilow in English class. The small building — the entire high school had only ninety-one students — was located next to Herziger's Slaughterhouse. Gene and Erna had trouble keeping their minds on what Miss Haden was saying about Shakespeare, Milton, Cowper, or Wordsworth, preferring to watch Herziger unloading cattle and leading them to their doom. Despite such distractions, Miss Haden gave him a respectable B minus in English. He might have rated a higher grade if his notebook had not been such a mess. "Strive for neatness," she scolded in handing it back. "Your notes are carelessly arranged."

William H. Fromm, the physics teacher, agreed that neatness was not his leading quality. Gene got a respectable grade of 80 on one paper he submitted, but Fromm described it as "shabby looking work" and ordered him to copy it over without a single error, "and neatly, without erasures. If you were not so awfully careless and shiftless in your work and in your reasoning," Fromm informed the future father of the Floribunda, "you could easily get a decent mark."

The senior play that year was entitled "Hicks at College," and Gene won the role of the leading man, Tom Horton. Lula Kroehnke was June,

Tom's girl. Horton was working his way through college. The climactic moment in the plot came when he had to choose whether to stay in school or take a $200-a-month job writing advertisements for Braino Breakfast Food. The audience was considerably relieved when Gene, as Tom, decided that education was more important than easy money and spurned the golden opportunity.

The high school's twelfth Commencement was held June 23, 1910 at Turner Hall, with Gene stepping forward with the other seniors to accept a diploma. That made him an alumnus, so he was entitled to go to the Alumni Ball, which began with "The Chanticleer Rag," a two-step, and ended promptly at midnight with another lively number called "Chung Lo."

In the fall of 1911 young Boerner went to Madison and enrolled in the University of Wisconsin's engineering school. Arthur arranged for Harry W. Bolens, his boss, to write a letter introducing Gene to a Madison friend, Guy Hinkel. "Help him get a room and look out a little for him," the president of Gilson Manufacturing urged Hinkel. "He is 100% pure stuff."

Gene rented a room at 608 West Dayton Street in Madison. Worried that he would get homesick, his family kept sending him cards and letters. He saved every one. Arthur, for example, wrote him on the stationery of a hotel in Eagle Lake, Texas — "The Drummer's home," rates $2.00 a day or $2.50 with bath — and described a fishing trip he and his brother, Herman, had just taken with the manager of the B.F. Avery & Sons Plow Co. of Dallas. They had spent the day on the Gulf of Mexico among porpoises, pelicans, and other wildlife that seemed quite exotic to a visitor from Wisconsin. Using hermit crabs for bait, Arthur caught a two-pound sheepshead and Herman pulled in a four-and-a-half pound redfish.

Miss Pawlik wrote long and motherly letters, scolding him for not writing more often, worrying about whether he'd caught cold. Arthur and Herman kept urging him to find a part-time job. Wearying of their exhortations, he finally found one washing dishes for his meals. The older brothers also complained that he wasn't taking college with the proper seriousness. They had cause for concern. His grades were poor. Somehow, he had even managed to flunk gym. "It would be a mighty poor record if you can't manage to clear up your marks before the year is up," Herman told him. "You certainly made a bum start and you can't afford to spoil it by monkeying around. It's up to you to make good. You can't afford to spend any extra time and money."

Boerner had started his college career full of boyish enthusiasm, and for a time he sent home glowing reports of life on the campus, where he was meeting new people and expanding horizons previously limited to those of a small, rather isolated town. But he soon discovered that engineering was not as interesting as he had expected. His classes seemed dull. His grades were a constant source of worry. After the first semester, he was put on probation ("conditioned" was the term used then). He didn't let it spoil his Christmas in Cedarburg; but when he got back to Madison, he made solemn resolves to do better. He had been having particular trouble with an English course. The mid-semester report issued on April 17 indicated that he had risen to a grade of "fair" in this subject. He was also evaluated as a fair student in German and drawing. But he was failing in math and mechanical drawing. The Freshman Mixer was scheduled a few days after this melancholy report, and Gene was not a lad to sulk in his room when there was mixing to be done. He skipped the first two dances, a two-step and a waltz. But then his courage or his luck improved, and he abandoned the stag line to dance with a Miss Mattean. From then on, judging from the variety of girls' names he meticulously noted on his program, the evening went well.

There was still the matter of those failing grades, however. He fretted about them for several weeks, but once he had made up his mind to leave Madison his departure was sudden. He stayed awake until 3 a.m., packed his belongings, then climbed out of bed two hours later to leave for Cedarburg. His arrival caught the family by surprise. Gene did not sit around the parlor brooding. There was a dance that night in Cedarburg, and he managed to arrange for a last-minute date with a girl named Livia. As a result, he wrote to Miss Pawlik, "my cup was full."

Still fulfilling his role as substitute father, Arthur decided to have a talk with this young college dropout. He knew how it was to have to leave the university. Arthur had attended for a year, intending to specialize in horticulture; but in 1907 with the family income ebbing, his father had suggested he take an office boy's job with the Gilson firm. This led to promotion to salesman and Arthur had never gone back to the university, but he had hoped his kid brother would stick it out. He and Gene sat under a tree in a little park near their home to discuss the situation. Arthur asked for an explanation of why Gene had come home.

"Art, I just don't think I'm cut out to be an engineer."

"Then what do you want to do?"

"I can't make up my mind. But engineering's not what I want."

The conversation went on for two hours. The brothers finally concluded that with a little more maturity, Gene might know better where he was going. He wrote Miss Pawlik to tell her what they'd decided. "The final conclusion was that I try to get some farm job for a few months and by that time I may have decided what I want. I have very nearly decided on something besides engineering. I don't know why, but it'll be something else." Not long afterward, Arthur called on a customer in Council Bluffs, Iowa, and mentioned that he had a young brother who needed a job. "Roy Wilcox has got the biggest greenhouse in the United States, right here in town," the customer told him. "They're always looking for help."

That sounded like just the thing for Gene, who already knew something about flowers. He got the job with J.F. Wilcox and Sons, which claimed to be "the largest greenhouse establishment west of the Mississippi," and off he went to Iowa. One of his first paychecks that fall

Gene Boerner at the age of twenty-one. His comment about this picture: "Please note faint shadows under nose. Sure sign of a beginning.... Am trying to train that 'cowlick' of mine into a 'pomp,' but it's slow work!"

was in error; the payment was higher than he was entitled to get. He called the overpayment to Wilcox's attention. When he told Arthur about it in his next letter, he was informed that he had done right but not to expect any special credit. "There is nothing particularly virtuous about just being honest," the older brother noted. "There should really never be any question on such a matter at all."

By the end of October, Gene had been promoted to the job of grower's helper, which entitled him to work thirteen days out of each fourteen, with every other Sunday off. He wrote to his Aunt Ida that he got up each morning at 5:45 and returned home at 6:45 p.m. The greenhouses where he was working, he told her, were worth $100,000, and "I wish they were mine." The work varied with the seasons. In December, when the temperature was ten degrees above zero, he was put to work clearing the top of the greenhouse of snow. The following August, he was working in the greenhouses when the temperature outside was ninety-eight degrees and he caught himself wishing he was back in Cedarburg. "When I hear those crickets chirping and the locusts whizzing and whirring and the frogs singing, with an occasional note from some frightened bird," he wrote Herman, "I can shut my eyes and imagine myself floating (alone!) down the creek."

He had been spreading bone meal during the heat wave. "It's stinky stuff at best but when you've got to remove most of your clothes or suffocate and then get it into every pore in your body — well, it isn't Utopia." When the cold weather came again, Eugene began to get restless. He toyed with the notion of giving up his job and heading west to see Yellowstone National Park. Herman urged him not to give in to such temptation "until you have got all they have to give you. This is your college course, so to speak, and you want to see that nothing of value gets by you."

Gene recognized that the advice was good. The spring of 1914 found him still in Council Bluffs, where he had celebrated his twenty-first birthday by starting to grow a mustache. "Maples are in full bloom and other buds are swelling," he wrote to his family in Cedarburg. "But all that looks mighty small. Why? My mustache now covers my upper lip."

Chapter V

Floating Over The Woods

Boerner's work in the Wilcox greenhouses was mostly menial, but it provided direction to his life. At last he had decided what he wanted to do. From that time forward he concentrated his energies on the raising, development, and promotion of flowers. During the summer of 1914 Gene returned to Cedarburg to work for the Cedar Hedge Farm Association, which had now been incorporated as a family business. He helped plant and cultivate forty thousand asters. His brother Herman was working at the farm for fifteen cents an hour. Presumably Gene's pay was the same.

When fall came, he headed for Champaign, Illinois, and enrolled in the University of Illinois, majoring in floriculture, a relatively new course of study. Illinois had just opened a Floriculture Building and had hired a few faculty members who were interested not only in growing flowers but in trying to improve them. Boerner soon made friends with Professor H.B. Dorner, whose enthusiasm was catching. Dorner encouraged Eugene to experiment with the hydridizing of chrysanthemums, a flower for which Boerner developed a particular enthusiasm because of a plan that was taking shape: He hoped to open his own florist's shop near the campus. It seemed to him that mums would sell well to the college crowd, and he paid close attention to whatever the professor had to say about them. Illinois was still a comparatively small university whose entrance requirements and scholastic standards, to Gene's way of thinking, were not as exacting as Wisconsin's. He kept up a busy correspondence not only with his numerous relatives but with girls in Madison and a young woman in Shreveport, Louisiana, Eva Marburg, who addressed him as "dear Buddy" and signed herself, "Sister."

During the dreary days of February, 1915, Gene decided to keep careful track of where his money went and started a daily log. His room cost $12 a month, his board $4.50 a week. During February he spent $20 for tuition, so that at the end of the month he had a balance of $60 on hand. "The only way to keep an accurate record is to keep a daily record," he had noted in the front of the book. "So here goes for a daily record this semester." By the end of March, however, the ledger noted gloomily that there was "no cash on hand." The entries stopped.

In 1916, his junior year, Boerner Brothers Manufacturing Association was liquidated and the assets distributed. Gene's share came to $468.83, a considerable fortune to him just then. He rented space for his florist's shop from the proprietor of Strauch's Photo Studio. It was located at 625 Wright Street in Champaign, directly opposite the university president's home on the campus. The student businessman took ads under the slogan, "E. S. Boerner, the Campus Florist — Flowers Delivered Anywhere." He sold roses for $1.00 to $1.50 a dozen, violets for $1.00 a bunch. During the fall he did a flourishing business in corsages for coeds and wives of alumni who turned out to watch the football team. The Red Grange era of football at Illinois was still several years ahead, but the sport drew fair-sized crowds to the home games and Boerner cashed in. Years later, when most college memories had grown dim, he still bragged: "I was the first man to put mums in football games in Illinois."

In December he reported happily to Aunt Ida that he'd sold twenty corsages for the Junior Prom at $2.00 to $2.50 each. Perhaps in celebration he sent a package of jams and jellies from the home farm to his Shreveport girl, following it with a shipment of flowers from his shop. She sent him a twelve-page letter of thanks. "There is no trait in a man which appeals to a woman more than thoughtfulness and consideration," she told him and in a subsequent letter enclosed a poem:

> I wish you would propose,
> I'm ready now and willing.
> There's not another man on earth
> For whom I care a shilling.

An answer to a hint like that was obviously necessary. Gene tried to compose a poem in reply, but it was hard going. Poetry was not his forte. The best he could do was one that began:

> Sis, your invitation is most kind,
> To know you I'll bind,
> Although I can't be there,
> I'll send a message through the air,
> And...

But inspiration left him. He stopped writing, although he carefully put the envelope on which he'd been scribbling away with his cherished papers. The long-distance romance cooled soon afterward; perhaps Gene was disillusioned with womankind when he sent asters and she wrote back thanking him for the lovely chrysanthemums. At any rate, Sis's letters became increasingly sisterly and before long stopped entirely.

On June 13, 1917, Gene and Albert H. Burger were the only graduates at Illinois' forty-sixth annual Commencement to receive degrees in floriculture. Nearly half a century later Boerner got a letter from S.B. Hutton, Jr., board chairman of the Conard-Pile Nurseries, reporting that he'd met Burger, who was "very proud of the fact that your half of the class had made a name for itself." At the moment, Gene took more satisfaction from knowing that he was the first of the boys in his family to get a college degree than in any hopes of glory to come. The future looked highly uncertain. Two months before his graduation, the United States had joined the Allies in what was then called the Great War. "I have a great fear that if I get into the war," he wrote to his family, "it will be at least three or four years before I can get near a florist's business again."

Like many other young men in those early months of World War I, however, he was quickly caught up in the excitement and patriotic fervor. He enlisted in the Army on October 13, 1917. When he was called for active duty nearly two months later, he volunteered for its air arm, joining that small band of daredevils who were ready to learn how to fly the flimsy biplanes then being used over France. It had been only fourteen years since the Wright brothers had proved it was possible to get an airplane off the ground. Going aloft was still a dangerous adventure. Gene had apparently never been up in a plane at the time he volunteered to fly one, but neither had most of the other youths who joined the Army Flying Corps.

Boerner was sent to aeronautical school in the "new state armory" on the Cornell University campus at Ithaca, New York. He and other would-be fliers lined up for typhoid shots, then were issued a mattress, mattress cover, slicker, overcoat, four blankets, and a pillow but no sheets, shoes, or uniform. The cadets made do with their civilian clothes until a new shipment of supplies arrived. Gene worried about flunking out of the eight-week course, which dealt with such things as engines and had nothing at all to do with floriculture. When he was graduated from ground school on February 9, 1918, he send word to his Aunt Ida that he was greatly relieved.

Before reporting to Camp Dick, located on the Fairgrounds in Dallas, Texas, he had a chance to spend a few weeks at home. He had his uniform by now, and he looked quite handsome. The neighborhood girls

Gene in a plane during his training in the U.S. Army Flying Corps at Ellington Field, Houston, Texas in 1918.

kept bringing him socks and sweaters they had knitted. Arthur and Herman's wives and his sister vied in preparing tempting meals for the young man who might soon be fighting in France. An older brother, William, was already there with the infantry. At Dallas, Gene was assigned to Squadron 9 and set about learning how to fly. By April 10, he was at Eberts Field in Lonoke, Arkansas, full of enthusiasm for his new life. "Flying is great," he wrote to Ida Boerner, and he told Herman: "To hell with your old Ford. I'd sooner hit a convection current up high, going over a woods, a road or a pond...I think of old Henry floating along on one wheel and I let her ride the waves."

An outbreak of malaria brought rumors that the United States Air Service planned to close the field. Gene was among those who caught the disease, its effect lingering for several years after he'd returned to civilian life. But by late May he was well enough to learn how to make his plane do tricks. His instructor took him a mile above the Arkansas countryside and demonstrated how to put the wood-and-canvas craft into a tailspin and bring it out again. Testing Boerner — "trying to get my goat," Gene said later — he put the plane into a vertical bank to the left, then the right, then the left again. When he saw that Gene was taking it all in stride, he yelled above the sound of the engine: "Take her, Boerner."

Gene put the plane into a tailspin. "I got some wonderful sensations and I gave the instructor some wonderful sensations," he wrote to Ida. "He turned around and asked me if I wanted to wipe us both off the map." The next maneuver went more smoothly, and soon Gene reported, "I enjoyed putting the ship into one spin after another until I couldn't think of much else than what I'd had for dinner. I managed to save myself, however."

Boerner had a close call when his plane's engine cut out as he was flying over the Gulf of Mexico, but he glided safely back to land. After seventy-two hours of flying time, he got his second lieutenant's commission in August, 1918, and was sent to Ellington Field near Houston. Another fifteen weeks of instruction in advanced flying, bombing, and aerial gunnery, and he would be ready for France. Looking ahead, Boerner decided he'd volunteer for daytime bombing runs instead of night flying. "In the daytime," he explained to Ida Boerner, "you have to fight off enemy planes, be shot at by archies and machine guns, and do anything from contact patrol work to actual bombing far in the interior. Me for it!"

A month after his arrival in Houston, however, the war was over. It was a letdown for the young man after all his preparations. But back home in Cedarburg his family was greatly relieved.

Instead of swooping over the enemy lines, Gene found himself a civilian again on January 18, 1919, and looking for work. He visited Arthur, then living in Dallas with his wife and young daughter, June, and found a job there at a greenhouse which had formerly been owned by a son of the eccentric millionaire, Hetty Green. Col. E.H.R. Green claimed to have spent $1,250,000 on the Dallas nursery operations but had tired of his expensive plaything six years before and sold out to a man named Miller. Gene described Miller as "a coffee and tea merchant who didn't know much about the business." By the time Boerner went to work there, Miller had died, the establishment was "pretty thoroughly run down," and the owner's widow was trying to get the place in shape so she could sell it.

The malaria that was his souvenir from his days in Arkansas made life difficult, but by dosing himself faithfully with quinine he was able to shake it. After the 1920 blooming season, Boerner picked two bushels of Rugosa seed pods, planning to dry them, take out the seeds, and bury them in sand so they could freeze during the winter and be ready for planting. At the time he expected to be in Texas for at least another year. But he was growing increasingly dissatified with his job, which offered no secure future, and later in 1920 he quit and went back to Cedarburg. He worked at his uncle's nursery and studied such trade publications as the *Florists Review,* where late in the year he saw an advertisement from a nursery in Newark, New York, not far from the Cornell campus where he had spent his early days with the Army. Jackson & Perkins had been having trouble in its greenhouses, where the plants were affected by several diseases new to the men working there. The company had decided it needed a college-trained assistant foreman and was willing to go as high as $14 a week to hire the right man.

Boerner knew that J. & P. was a leading wholesaler of plants, particularly roses. He wrote a letter of application, saying he wanted to work for the best company in the business. Back came a reply suggesting he make his way to Newark and talk about it. The company had been started in 1872 as an informal partnership between an attorney, Charles H. Perkins, and his father-in-law, A. E. Jackson. Perkins' hobby was gardening, and he raised strawberries, raspberries, and blackberries for the nearby fruit markets. When Jackson & Perkins was organized, it was largely a one-man operation, with Perkins selling plants to his Newark neighbors and to nurserymen in the Finger Lake district of northern New York State.

Among the little firm's customers was the Ellwanger & Barry Nurseries in Rochester, one of whose owners, H. B. Ellwanger, wrote a book called *The Rose.* Perkins read it, and it fired his ambition to get into the rose-growing business. In 1884 he hired E. Alvin Miller, who had learned the techniques of rose propagation in his native Germany. Additional land was purchased or leased, another greenhouse was built — its windows were bought from a local church which was being rebuilt — and the berry gardeners went into the rose business.

J. & P. was still a small operation. The office work was conducted in the library of Perkins' home, with a neighbor woman keeping the books and answering letters when she wasn't too busy with housekeeping. Perkins regarded the nursery as a sideline to his other activities. Among those who helped out during the busy summers were three teenage sons of his brother Herbert, who lived in Grand Rapids, Michigan.

In 1892, when George C. Perkins graduated from college, he joined his father's business. It was then taking in only about $10,000 a year, was operating from a single small greenhouse and a nursery area of about thirty acres. George plunged into his new job with enthusiasm. He expanded the operations, adding more land, a larger greenhouse, and additional plantings, with fruit trees and roses the specialties. Jackson, who had never been active in the firm, died three years later, and Charles Perkins turned over increasing responsibility to his son and nephews.

Miller, who was a foreman as well as plant propagator, experimented with hybridizing roses, crossing two varieties in the hope that an improved rose would result. One of his experiments was the crossing of a variety called Mme. Gabriel Luizet with Rosa Wichuraiana. Of the twenty-five seedlings which resulted, one turned out to be a pink climber, its blossoms carried in clusters. Named Dorothy Perkins after the owner's granddaughter, this rose won the Nickerson Cup, presented by the National Rose Society of England in 1908. It was, for a time, the most widely-grown climber in the world. Travelers sent word back to Newark that they'd seen it in Australia, in Persia, in China or India. In 1913 a visitor to England told J. & P. he'd seen "miles of pillars in the Windsor Castle estate with Dorothy Perkins plants that in some instances grew as high as twenty feet."

All of this was encouraging and, to some extent, profitable. But the time when a new rose could be patented and royalties charged for its reproduction was still some years away. So many of the Dorothy Perkins climbers which were spreading so prolifically in distant places brought not a penny of profit to the rose's originators. Still, it was due in part to the enormous success of Dorothy Perkins that the company's business expanded. By the time Boerner arrived from Texas to apply for a job, J. & P. had an annual gross income of close to a million dollars. Its nursery area had grown to a thousand acres. It was wholesaling its plants in many parts of the United States and Canada.

When Gene got to Newark, he had a talk with George Perkins, by now president and treasurer of the firm. Then he was turned over to Jacob Catteau — the name was sometimes spelled Cattoo — who was superintendent of the greenhouses and something of a character. Jake was a grizzled but vigorous two hundred pounder who'd begun working for the company as a small boy who spent summers weeding the gardens. Not content with a six-day week, he now had the habit of hopping on his bicycle on Sundays to wheel off to the greenhouses to make sure the plants were still flourishing. After half a century as a Jackson &

Perkins employee, Catteau had the notion the roses wouldn't grow without him.

Old Jake motioned to young Gene to follow him on a tour of the nursery operations. The inspection wound up in the sheds where young women were busily transferring plants into clay pots, ready to be sent to florists. Catteau walked to the end of one of the benches. He pointed to a large pile of fresh cow manure.

"Grab a handful of that stuff," Jake ordered.

Borner had on his best suit, a white shirt and tie for the job interview. But he didn't hesitate. He picked up a fistful. The old man still wasn't satisfied.

"Now squeeze it."

Boerner did as he was told. Old Jake studied him for a moment. Then he nodded.

"All right. Throw it back in the pile and go wash your hands."

"Can I ask you something, Mr. Catteau? What did you have me do that for?

Jake glowered at him, but there was a twinkle in his eye.

"You claim you're a nurseryman," he said. "I just wanted to be sure you were willing to work with that stuff."

Chapter VI

Learning From Dr. Nicolas

Thanks in part to his farm boy familiarity with a product that made the roses grow and to his willingness to get his hands dirty, Boerner was hired. It turned out to be a lucky decision for him, for Jackson & Perkins, and for the future progress of the rose. In 1920, when Gene became an assistant foreman, J. & P. was little known outside the florists' trade. It was a plant wholesaler whose salesmen covered territories that included all parts of the country except the deep South and the far West, but it had no dealings with the general public.

By that year, Charles H. Perkins, the founder, had retired to a California orange grove, where he kept busy by running a poultry ranch. The business was in the hands of his son, George, and three nephews — Charles H. Perkins II was the vice-president, Clarence was in charge of the sales staff and spent much of his time on the road, and Ralph worked as a salesman. Another nephew, Carroll Perkins, joined the family business some years later.

Besides the company's extensive holdings in Newark, a prosperous village on the New York State Barge Canal, it had added a branch nursery near Bridgeton, New Jersey, to produce boxwood, azaleas, rhododendrons, and other specialties. These had been imported from Holland until a federal regulation, Quarantine Number 37, cut off American nurseries from foreign sources of supply. There was no rule against importing nurserymen, however, and a young Dutchman named De Wilde had been brought to Bridgeton to take charge of operations there.

The quarantine against foreign-grown plants proved a disguised blessing for such companies as Jackson & Perkins by forcing them to grow their own plants and, to a larger extent than before, develop their own varieties. Even before the drying up of foreign sources the Newark firm had preferred to propagate most of its own plants, but the quarantine encouraged the Perkins family to expand their production. By the time Boerner joined the firm, it was selling more than a quarter of a million rose bushes a year, along with such other specialties as evergreens, hydrangeas, and clematis — in all, nearly two million plants annually. Its storage cellars contained three million young plants to be put in the nursery the following spring. It kept a herd of cattle at its barns each winter, mostly as a ready source of organic fertilizer, although the company tried to make a profit when it sold the animals in the spring.

Boerner hit it off with George Perkins, his new boss, from the first. Two months after he got to Newark, Perkins invited him to go along on a trip to New York City. It was the young man's first visit to the big town, and Perkins made it a point to show him the sights. They rode to the top of the city's tallest skyscraper, the Woolworth Building. They visited the Brooklyn Bridge. They dined at fine restaurants, mingled with the hurrying crowds on the streets, stayed up late talking about the future of the rose business. "I slept only three or four hours a night," Gene reported proudly to his family back in Cedarburg.

The family was changing. Helene had married the Rev. E. Benjamin Schlueter, a pastor who would later become the president of the Evangelical Lutheran Synodical Conference in America. The bride had taken her three youngest brothers to live with her, with Miss Pawlik moving on to become governess for children of a member of the Pabst Brewing clan at Oconomowoc, Wisconsin. Then, in June of 1922, the old days were ended for good. Gene got a telegram. His grandmother, Oma, had died. Cedar Hedge farm was still in the family and there were plenty of Boerners left in the old home town, but Cedarburg was never the same to him after that.

By now the Boerners were engaged in a variety of occupations. Arthur was still working as a salesman. William farmed for a while, then got a job with a manufacturing firm. Helene had taught school in Markesan, Wisconsin, after her graduation from Milwaukee-Downer College in Milwaukee as a dietitian, before getting married. Robert Louis Stevenson Boerner, named for one of his father's favorite authors, was graduated from the University of Wisconsin's College of Agriculture and became a county agent in South Dakota before becoming a Milwaukee landscaper. He and his brothers Arthur and Herman later started a small landscaping business in Milwaukee, but the other two brothers dropped out and Robert operated it by himself. Alfred, who followed Gene's example and attended the University of Illinois, graduated with a degree in landscape architecture and was to go on to become general manager of the Milwaukee County park system and a nationally-known landscaper. Carl, the youngest, was to get his law degree at Wisconsin and become an attorney.

Learning From Dr. Nicolas

As a newcomer at J.&P., Gene soon was accepted by the oldtimers, those who had fifteen to as much as fifty years with the company. It seemed more like a family group than a coldly-commercial sort of business. The custom of giving each employee with more than a year's service a ten per cent bonus at Christmas helped build this loyalty, but the work was interesting. Although the hours were long and the chores sometimes tedious, the turnover of employees was not a serious problem.

The work week was fifty-four hours — nine hours a day, six days a week — plus additional duty every third Sunday. Until shortly before Boerner was hired, the men had put in ten-hour days. Being able to quit after only nine hours was considered an improvement. There were drawbacks to the job, however. The greenhouses got so hot in the summer that some of the workmen ate their lunches in full sun so they needn't get used to the heat again when they went back inside. Two years after he got there, Gene decided he wasn't advancing rapidly enough. He sounded out Conard & Jones Co. of West Grove, Pennsylvania, about a job. He was told that his prospects were minimal just then.

In 1923, the firm's fiftieth anniversary year, it was specializing in roses, but not many of the names in its catalogue would be familiar to modern gardeners. One of its biggest sellers was La France, the first important hybrid tea, which had been introduced by a French hybridizer only two years after the end of the American Civil War. Most of the early hybrid teas were considered too tender for outdoor culture in the northern states — "Hybrid Perpetuals" were the usual roses for outdoor gardening — but by now a number of varieties had been introduced which were said to be suitable for northern climates, among them Aladdin, Angelus, Benedicte Seguin, and British Queen. Jackson & Perkins also was offering a hybrid tea class called Pernetiana, although admitting that these were of no more mixed parentage than many of the older kinds and perhaps did not deserve a special classification. M. Pernet-Ducher, the French hybridist, had crossed the Austrian Briar with the hybrid tea, producing new hues and qualities in such roses as Beauté de Lyon. A surprising number of the varieties being sold in 1923 dated back to the mid-nineteenth century. One, an Austrian Briar credited to Gerard, had originated in 1596. The catalogue also offered climbers, moss roses, and Eglantine or Sweetbriars.

That was the year when George Perkins decided he'd had enough of traveling as the company's chief salesman. He picked Boerner to take over that job when he wasn't too busy with his duties at the greenhouses. Salesmanship was not the career Gene had trained for at the University of Illinois, but the change suited him. He liked to move around from city to city, talking with the florists, making friends, seeing new places. His territory, he liked to point out in later years, was "from Maine to Florida," but he spent most of his time in New England. He liked the travel. All his adult life he was a man who hated to stay long in one spot and was always ready to pack his bag and be off. He was younger than most of the florists he met in this phase of his career, but he had an ideal background for dealing with them. He had grown up in a family of small town businessmen, so he understood the talk of prodits and loss. From experience in his uncle's nursery and his days as a campus florist, he understood the problems of raising and selling flowers and nursery stock. Besides, he was a gregarious man who enjoyed meeting people and shooting the breeze.

Boerner's work as a salesman kept him on the road much of the year, but when the busy season began at the greenhouses he returned to Newark to help with the hybridizing and make himself otherwise useful. "When the horse chestnuts bloomed in New England, I knew I had to hurry back to the office," he would say in describing those days. He seldom returned emptyhanded from his New England travels. He might bring back a barrel of raw oysters, then telephone some of his cronies and arrange a feast. One year he returned with a jar of lobster liver. Not wanting to tackle this untested delicacy alone, he called up Charles Baldwin, the J. & P. office manager, who came to his apartment. They discovered by spreading the liver on French toast that it was delicious.

During such interludes from salesmanship, Boerner joined in what he later described as Jackson & Perkins' pioneering efforts to start the budded rose business. Until then greenhouse roses had been propagated by grafting the cultivated varieties on hardy root stocks. About 1925 Boerner and others at J.& P. decided there might be a better way. Instead of using grafts, the roses would be budded. "At that time," Gene noted fifteen years later, "Briarcliff, Premier, White Killarney and Richmond were the principal varieties in use. Foreign Manetti was imported and planted in the fields at Newark. These stocks were then budded and the plants dug in fall and sold as dormant eyes. This idea was good but there were too many of the buds which either did not start at all or started very irregularly, giving uneven benches which were not profitable."

Learning From Dr. Nicolas

The experiment might have been written off as a failure, but Boerner noticed that those plants which did grow were more vigorous plants than the ones produced by the old grafting method. It was decided to try to start the eye in the field by cutting the top off the plants after budding. "This method worked better," Boerner said. "But now we found our growing season was too short in New York State to mature these plants and we found that pre-rooted Manetti gave us a two-year root system, which was not as quickly responsive when planted in the greenhouses' benches. Since these plants did not mature soon enough there again developed trouble in the benches, even though the started eyes did give a much bushier plant in a shorter period."

At this point the operations were moved to California, where the long growing season made it possible to grow the ideal budded plant. It was started from a cutting made in the spring. The cutting was budded and branched, then dug later the same year. Because the roots were first-year growth, they would quickly send out new rootlets and take hold vigorously when planted by the grower. The tops were branched and full of young basal eyes, ready to start the vigorous base shoots necessary for heavy bench production soon after planting.

"This combination of root and top," Boerner noted, "has given the Triple X grade started buds definitely the top position in the bud world. The grower seldom needs more than two pinches to bring his plants into crop. After that, he gets heavy production. The started plants have eliminated the danger of loss through eyes breaking out or rotting, which used to occur in the old-fashioned dormant eyes after the end of April. We have definitely eliminated the old idea that budded plants cannot be planted after the end of April." All of this took a long period of experimentation, fifteen years which Boerner said were "hard, expensive and sometimes almost heartbreaking." But the end result was improved stock for J. & P.'s greenhouse customers which boosted the company's share of that important market.

In the years when Boerner was dividing his time between floriculture and salesmanship, this budding experiment was only beginning. By 1925 he was earning $5,500 a year in salary, bonuses, and commissions, enough to be able to put money aside for the future. The federal tax on that income, it may be noted with nostalgia for days now gone, was exactly $7.51.

When an opportunity to buy into the business arrived three years later, Gene was ready to take advantage of it. After thirty-five years with the firm, George C. Perkins had decided to sell his interest in the company his father had founded. Boerner became a part owner, along with three of the founder's nephews, Charles, Clarence, and Ralph Perkins, and the company's secretary, Paul V. Fortmiller. After the latter's death, Gene took over the title of secretary and the ownership was realigned, with each of the four surviving owners picking up a larger share. During the years of the company's greatest growth, Boerner and Ralph Perkins each owned twelve per cent of the stock, Clarence Perkins held twenty-five per cent, and Charles Perkins had the controlling interest, fifty-one per cent.

As the principal owner, Charles Perkins became president of the company in 1928. The founder's nephew and namesake had first worked in the nursery when he was twelve years old, being hired as a helper there after his uncle paid a visit to his farm home near Grand Rapids to point out the opportunities for a likely lad in the rose business. Young Charles' father was an honest man, and he felt it only fair to warn his brother that young Charles had started to smoke before his twelfth birthday, so might come to no good end. But Uncle Charles was willing to overlook this evidence of the devil's work. He put his nephew to work cleaning the Newark stables. From that chore he graduated to the fields, where he learned the drudgery and the rewards of horticulture. The younger Charles became the company's first salesman, setting out by train or horse and buggy to visit florists in 1908. Twenty years later, when he became the president and chief stockholder, he'd had practical experience in all the company's operations and was ready to expand.

The company had done some plant research ever since 1884, but the new president decided to put greater emphasis on the development of new varieties. He hired an internationally-known French hybridist as head of the research department. Dr. Jean Henri Nicolas, who arrived in 1930, was a graduate of the military college of Saint Cyr and had been the youngest captain in the French Army until an injury forced him to retire from military service. He turned to horticulture and soon was a leading expert in that field. His book, *The Rose Manual*, became a standard reference book in English-speaking countries.

At the time Nicolas arrived, Perkins and other growers recognized that they were on the eve of a profound change in the rose business. Prompted by some vigorous and persistent lobbying by nurserymen, with Boerner taking a leading role in this behind the scenes activity in Washington, Congress had at last been persuaded to pass a law which would make it possible for the originator of a plant variety to patent it and collect royalties. Perkins hired the French hybridist to be ready to cash in. Without the patent law's protection there had been little reason for an extensive hybridization program. It was cheaper to let the Europeans originate new roses, a long and expensive process. Most American nurserymen had been content to import the new varieties, then propagate them. The patent law of 1931 changed this. With Nicolas in charge, Jackson & Perkins was ready. Boerner was still primarily a salesman, but when he wasn't on the road, he worked with the hybridist and learned from him.

Nicolas' reputation — France made him a Knight of the Legion of Honor in 1931 — opened doors for J. & P. abroad. He was able to mingle on an equal footing with such European rose hybridizers as Wilhelm Kordes, whose nursery at Sparrieshoop in Germany was a consistent source of improved rose strains, and Kordes' neighbor, Mathias Tantau. Now that the patent law had been passed, J. & P. and other American nurserymen were also trying to create their own new varieties which could be sold without paying a royalty to outside hybridists.

As Nicolas pointed out in his book, *The Rose Manual*, the originators of a new rose — or any other plant, for that matter — had been given no protection before the patent law was passed "beyond their own means of concealing it and accumulating a stock before putting it on the market," so that when other commercial growers got hold of the novelty they could "propagate and sell it at any price they chose without obligation to the originator."

Nicolas predicted that passage of the patent law would encourage many amateur growers to take up rose hybridization, "knowing that any worthy novelty born from their handiwork will be protected and may become a source of revenue." He did not need to add that the law also gave such companies as J. & P. a financial incentive to originate and patent a seemingly endless succession of new varieties.

At the time Nicolas was hired, there was a fundamental difference in attitude between American and European rose growers. The schism is illustrated by the history of the annual rose shows where varieties competed against each other for prizes and recognition. In the United States, except for local contests among amateur gardeners, the shows were sponsored and patronized by professional florists, which meant that little attention was paid to how well a rose would do in the home garden. The gold medal varieties were suitable for greenhouse culture. Their ability to perform well out-of-doors was then of no concern.

In Europe the roses exhibited had been grown in the open, and amateur gardeners often walked off with the prizes. However, most of the shows held there featured only cut flowers, not plants. Hence, Nicolas said, a European prizewinner might not be "worth a whoop as far as garden roses go" because "exhibition roses seldom are good garden roses."

Like most rose enthusiasts, Nicolas felt that the place for the flower was in a well-designed garden, but many of the more desirable varieties were not hardy in the north. In such states as Michigan and Wisconsin and in portions of Pennsylvania, Ohio, and even northern Arizona, Nicolas advised that only Rugosa, some of its hybrids, and those wild roses native to the regions were reliably hardy. Shrub roses had been carried west by the pioneers, and most home gardeners in 1930 had a few of these June-flowering bushes, but the less-common varieties were considered merely hothouse flowers to be used in florists' bouquets or to be sold as pot plants for some special occasion, such as Easter.

Boerner recognized Nicolas' arrival as an opportunity to learn about rose hybridization from a recognized master. The two men quickly became friends. As the scholarly-looking Frenchman worked around the greenhouse or walked along the rows in the test gardens — somehow managing to maintain his dignity while wearing knickers — Gene asked questions and paid respectful attention to the answers. Hybridization, Nicolas told him, was not so much a science as an art. A successful hybridizer needed imagination, the gift of observation, unlimited patience. He also needed something else, Nicolas said: An honest love of roses.

Sometimes on their early morning walks the talk turned to the history of rose-breeding. Until the early nineteenth century, Nicolas pointed out, new varieties had been produced mostly by chance. Gardeners interested in improving the breed had planted seeds more or less at random, then watched for a plant that varied in a desirable way from its parents.

"But then came the Empress Josephine," the Frenchman said. "Whatever you may think of Napoleon, we must give his empress credit, eh, Gene?"

"I'd like to visit her roseraie of Malmaison some day."

"It's not the same as in her time, of course. Still, you must see it when you go to France. About twenty years ago Jules Gravereaux finished assembling ninety of the two hundred fifty varieties that were there in Josephine's day. But after a century many of them had disappeared for good."

Learning From Dr. Nicolas

Josephine's ambition as a gardener was one that only an empress would have been able to accomplish in 1810. She sought to grow at least one example of every known rose in the world. More significantly, she hired botanists and nurserymen and ordered them to produce new varieties. It was one of her men, André Dupont, who first practiced hand pollination, a method that ended the practice of leaving the production of new varieties strictly to chance. "I found a reference to old André in a French journal published in 1811," Nicolas told Boerner. "I like what the writer called him: 'An enchanter who submits the rose to his magic wand and forces it to undergo the most surprising and agreeable transformation.' "

Hybridizers might be in the enchantment business, but it was plain to Boerner that they also must be practical men who took pains to produce roses which were not only beautiful but had other qualities sought by customers. In the case of the greenhouse operators who were J. & P.'s usual buyers, it was necessary that the rose be a continuous bloomer, capable of "forcing," of being brought into bloom at a time when the market was at its height. Among the favorites for this purpose in the mid-twenties were Souvenir de Claudius Pernet, Francis Scott Key, and Premier, varieties which were of little value to the home gardener.

The florists' trade was hard hit by the Depression of the 1930s. Many families were having too much trouble keeping food on the table to spend money on hot house plants or cut flowers. Despite the hard times, however, home gardeners with plenty of time on their hands continued to buy plants. If a family wanted roses, it was cheaper to grow their own than to buy bouquets. So Nicolas not only tried to develop new varieties that would appeal to the retail garden shops' customers but also made annual trips to Europe to seek the best new roses which had been created there. By the mid-thirties, Boerner sometimes substituted for him on these European scouting expeditions.

W. Kordes Sohne's Crimson Glory, a cross between a Cathrine Kordes seedling and a hybrid tea, W. E. Chaplin, proved to be the hit of the 1935 season. Henry Dreer & Co. of Philadelphia introduced it in the United States, but within a few months Charles Perkins bought the patent rights and cashed in on its triumph.

By now some of Nicolas' crosses were ready for the market, too, and in 1935 his yellow hybrid tea won a gold medal at the International Rose Test Gardens in Portland, Oregon, and another gold medal in Rome. The following year it was honored at the Bagatelle show in Paris. Eclipse had first bloomed during an eclipse on August 31, 1932, hence the name.

With Nicolas in charge of research and the Perkins brothers and Boerner taking care of the business and salesmanship duties, J. & P. expanded rapidly despite the hard times. One cloud on this successful arrangement was Nicolas' health. He became ill, with Boerner temporarily taking over his duties. Even after his apparent recovery he needed to husband his strength. When it came time for the 1937 buying trip to Europe, he asked Gene to make it for him. This suited Boerner fine; there was nothing he liked better than to hurry off to meet new people and talk about roses.

One of his first stops was at the Royal Horticultural Society's show in Olympia Hall, London. He found the English very businesslike. Most of those attending were on the hunt for new and different plants for their gardens. The tradesmen were doing a fine business, booking orders for the fall and spring. He noted that the fall coloring of the English countryside was much like that of northern New York. "It is very heartening to see staid businessmen carrying bunches of Michaelmas daisies in the streets of London," he reported that fall. "Flowers are a more intimate part of the life of the English who are, fortunately, not so self-conscious as we in expressing their appreciation of them."

At the Paris Exposition he took special note of the espaliered trees which were the dominant display in the outdoor plantings. Most of the trees had already shed their leaves. He felt that they had been planted too late; they should have been put in place at least a year in advance so that they would have become well established before the show.

In Germany he was impressed by the popularity of a new class of roses which he called floribundas. "Municipalities planted as many as ten thousand of one variety," he wrote, "making a lavish display of massed color. Private individuals are using them not only in their rose beds but in private foundation plantings, perennial borders and shrub borders.

"This suggests to me that we Americans could do well to liberalize our views regarding the use of roses. Why not incorporate them with other plantings about the home premises, rather than restricting them to the rose garden?

"The floribunda group, intermediary between the hybrid tea and the polyantha, is particularly adaptable to landscape use and is quickly finding its place and justifying its existence. Among many people of our country who have not previously been successful with roses, I predict a great future for the more easily-cultivated floribunda branch of the rose family."

Jackson & Perkins was already offering a number of floribundas — Anne Poulsen, Carillon, White Grüss an Aachen, Snowbank, Permanent Wave, Else Poulsen, Golden Main, and several others. Boerner was convinced they were ideal for amateur growers. "Floribunda is a group especially bred for mass planting and garden decoration," he wrote that fall of 1937. "It is the development of an idea evolved from the necessity of having an intermediary group between the very rugged, small-flowered polyanthas and the large-flowered hybrid teas. The floribunda is a group, not a strain, because these roses are derived from various Arctic species sources." The floribundas had sturdy, hardy, very bushy plants of medium height, he noted, combining the continuous blooming habit of the polyanthas with the large flowers of the tea roses.

Touring the floribunda displays in Germany with such growers as Kordes and Tantau, he was impressed with the way the flowers retained their shape and color even in the hottest summer. But as a native of a cold climate, he was even more enthusiastic about their hardiness. "The rose is preeminently a garden flower, and this new group brings it more closely to the perennial status in garden ornamentation," he wrote to rose enthusiasts back home.

Some of the varieties J. & P. was now calling floribundas had previously been classed as either hybrid polyanthas or hybrid teas. Boerner, as well as Nicolas and the Perkins brothers, considered them distinctive enough to be given a more descriptive designation, one which was, not incidentally, potentially more profitable if gardeners could be persuaded that floribundas would solve some of their long-standing problems with roses in difficult climates.

In September, with Nicolas still in charge of the hybridizing program at Newark and with Boerner abroad, the Frenchman felt well enough to make a tour of rose centers in the Eastern United States. Midway on the trip, he became ill again. On September 25, 1937, he died. The word reached Boerner in Paris. It meant a new opportunity had opened to him to head the company's hybridizing program, but the news left him with a feeling of depression. He had been fond of Nicolas. He would miss those 6 a.m. sessions in the rose gardens, when he and Perkins and the Frenchman had walked past rows of flowers at an hour when they could catch them in the first flush of their beauty. Sitting there in Paris, Gene could still recall Nicolas' enthusiasm as he exclaimed over the soft blendings of colors which the midsummer heat had not yet had a chance to transform.

Boerner continued his trip, bringing the news of Nicolas' death to old friends and associates in Europe. They found it fitting that, after the funeral, his ashes had been scattered in a bed of his favorite roses. As soon as he had finished buying the plants which seemed most likely to prove profitable in the United States, Boerner hurried back to Newark. Charlie Perkins gave him his instructions: "You're our head hybridizer now, Gene. After fifteen years on the road, you know what we need. Now get out your camel's hair pollen brush and produce it."

Chapter VII

Birth Of The Floribunda

When Gene Boerner took over for Dr. Nicolas as the company's research director, he came to the job with what proved to be an ideal background for a new era that was approaching in both rose production and rose marketing. He not only had the practical and scientific training needed to become a pre-eminent breeder of new roses, but his years as a traveling salesman for the nursery meant he also knew the practicalities of marketing them. Like Charlie Perkins, he was both a flower lover and a flower promoter, a combination which proved to be exactly what Jackson & Perkins needed to become the world's largest producer of roses.

One of Boerner's first tasks was to decide which rose hybridized by his predecessor should be named after him. Gene and Perkins agreed on a pink climber, a cross Nicolas had made between roses named Charles P. Kilham and Georg Arends. As the Dr. J.H. Nicolas, this rose was introduced three years after its originator's death. By then, J. & P. was no longer confining itself to the wholesale business. The change came about more or less by happenstance.

In their role as promoters as well as growers and sellers, the Perkins brothers and Boerner decided that the New York World's Fair taking shape in Flushing Meadows offered a fine opportunity to encourage visitors to go back home and buy plants from those florists and nurseries that were supplied by Jackson & Perkins. The company already claimed to produce more rose bushes than any of its rivals — over five million a year — and J. & P. was a logical choice to create a display which would benefit the entire flower-selling industry. It decided to take over a ten-thousand-square-foot plot of ground on the fairgrounds and to display eight thousand blooming rose bushes in a garden to be called "The Parade of Modern Roses." The rose garden was part of a six-acre area set aside to show the progress of horticulture under the sponsorship of the Society of American Florists, the New York Florists' Club, and the New York Horticultural Club.

A Columbia University professor, Hugh Findlay, was assigned to design the rose garden. In consultation with Boerner and other J. & P.

officials, he divided it into three sections. One was given over to hybrid teas from Ireland, France, Belgium, Holland, and Germany, with such yellow varieties as McGredy's Sunset, Alice Harding, and Amelia Earhart featured. Another section included roses from Italy, Spain, Holland, Denmark, Switzerland, England, and America, with one bed devoted to varieties so new they were not yet named.

Between these sections, featuring the familiar hybrid teas, was an area planted entirely with the roses which, against some well-entrenched opposition, Jackson & Perkins insisted on calling floribundas. Boerner gave special attention to choosing the varieties included in this display. He included Grüss an Aachen, Betty Prior, Donald Prior, Permanent Wave, Joyous, Summer Snow, Smiles, Rochester, and a rose which its originator had called the Minna Kordes. At Gene's suggestion Wilhelm Kordes was willing to have Minna's flowery namesake called World's Fair for the American market. Most of the floribundas were of European origin, but Smiles and Rochester had been hybridized by Nicolas. The garden provided a sort of living history of the floribunda for those familiar with its background.

The Holland import named Joyous was a sport of Else Poulsen, which had been hybridized by a Danish pioneer in the development of the floribunda named Svend Poulsen. The Donald and Betty Prior varieties were also descendants of Poulsen strains, hybridized in England to produce taller and more vigorous bushes. As for Kordes, originator of World's Fair, he had helped develop and popularize the floribunda in Germany. Some of his varieties would serve as ancestral stock for dozens of prize-winning floribundas Boerner was to develop.

"Contrary to general belief," Svend Poulsen wrote to Gene in describing the early history of the floribunda, "there was no fixed idea behind the first hybridizing, which was carried on at the beginning of this century by my eldest brother, Dines Poulsen." Dines had crossed a baby rambler named Mme. Norbert Levavasseur with an everblooming jack rose called Richmond. The result was a hybrid he called Rodhaette, one of the first floribundas, which appeared on the market in 1911. Dines Poulsen also crossed Levavasseur with Dorothy Perkins, the rambler which had helped Boerner's company expand. This combination produced a rose he called Ellen Poulsen, a floribunda introduced the same year as Rodhaette. "These were the first he selected for distribution, not knowing their real value, their hardiness, and many other good qualities, which we found out about later," Svend Poulsen told Boerner.

Svend took over the hybridizing during World War I. As reports begin to reach him of the floribunda's hardiness and free-flowering habit, he increased his efforts to improve the strain. In 1924 he introduced two more floribundas, Else Poulsen and Kirsten Poulsen. "It was really the appearance of Else Poulsen that made the breeders outside of Denmark conscious of the value of this new type of rose," Svend told Gene. "When Queen Mary selected Else Poulsen as her favorite rose, even the conservative English public began to notice it. From then on, hybridizing of (floribunda) roses increased, not alone by our firm but everywhere — Kordes, Tantau, Krause, in France, Holland, England, and the U.S.A. The increase in floribunda crossings is still going on, and from what I have seen, everybody seems to want to transform the floribunda to grandiflora and even to hardy, rich-flowering hybrid teas."

Wilhelm Kordes had his own ideas about the floribunda's back-

Wilhelm Kordes, a rose hybridizer from Spar-rieshoop, Germany and a close friend of Gene Boerner.

ground. It was his belief — and Boerner agreed — that the first floribunda predated the elder Poulsen's experiments, being introduced in 1900, when Peter Lambert, a German, crossed a polyantha named Mignonette and a tea rose, Souvenir de Mme. Savlayrolles, to produce a variety he called Schneekopf. Kordes told Gene of the early history of his own work with floribundas. He started the Rosa multibracteata, which had been brought to Europe from China. Mathias Tantau, his neighbor, also started to experiment with this rose about 1910. Meanwhile, Kordes continued to use the sweetbriar in his experiments, which gave "very good results."

"In the run of generations," Kordes went on, "I succeeded in getting repeat-flowering forms. From these we bred our floribundas. I also bred from the repeat-flowering Moschata strain, derived from Lambert's Trier via Robin Hood from (the Rev. J. H.) Pemberton. The syntheses of these strains are our floribundas of today. It took some hundred pollinations to get a repeat-flowering sweetbriar, dwarf and hardy, and from these I could breed further. The same applies to the Moschata hybrids. The original cross gave two seedlings, Eva and Skyrocket, both free and hardy and resistant to black spot. One of the repeat-flowering floribunda types was Rosenmarchen (Pinocchio). Nearly fifty per cent of the modern floribundas hail from this variety.

"I wanted frost hardiness. I wanted resistance to black spot and also (I wanted) repeat flowering. A little bit has been realized — and, of course, there must always be something left for the breeders of tomorrow."

Before his death Nicolas began working with floribundas, with Boerner an interested observer and helper in his experiments, which produced varieties called Snowbank, Smiles,and Rochester. "Rochester is a seedling of the polyantha Echo and the Rev. F. Page Roberts," Boerner noted. "In this way, Doctor Nicolas kept the floriferousness of the polyantha and brought in some of the larger size of the Rev. F. Page Roberts. One candelabra of blooms with as many as sixty flowers has been reported for this variety."

Boerner was not yet ready in the late thirties to talk about his own hybridizing efforts, which would produce finer floribundas than any that had gone before. But he was willing to make a prediction: "With the greater use of the floribunda, a new field for roses is opened in every garden. With these plants it will be possible for everyone to have roses and to have cut flowers in their homes. The colder regions will be able to enjoy them."

Within twenty years of this prediction, floribundas had surpassed the hybrid teas, and Boerner deserved a considerable share of the credit for changing a nation's gardening habits. "Without Jackson & Perkins, the floribunda would not be what it is today," a *New Yorker* reporter declared in a 1958 article, "and without the floribunda Jackson &

Perkins might be just another nursery."

The name "floribunda" was originated by J. & P. It was created because the notion that an average rose grower would be attracted by a class called "polyanthus hybrids" or "large-flowered polyanthas" ran counter to the selling experience of the Perkins brothers and that old New England rose salesman, Gene Boerner. The search began for a less unwieldy title. Suggestions were considered and discarded. Finally, a visiting writer on horticultural topics strolled past the flower beds in Newark, admiring the multiplicity of blooms, and asked: "Why not call it 'floribunda,' which means 'many-flowered'?" And so floribunda it became, at least around Jackson & Perkins. The American Rose Society did not agree. The society had the responsibility for grading and recording all new roses, and it told Charlie Perkins the name was not acceptable.

For one thing, floribunda was the name given by nineteenth-century French hybridists to two varieties which now were extinct. Besides, floribunda was the obsolete botanical name of two species of roses.

"Then what do you want us to call it?" Perkins demanded.

"Call it 'large-flowered hybrid polyanthas'."

The Perkins brothers and Boerner considered the ruling ridiculous. It was hard to imagine anyone going to a neighborhood nursery and asking for a "large-flowered hybrid polyantha." In the interests of both clarity and salesmanship they decided to defy the society's order. Jackson & Perkins went ahead and advertised floribundas in its catalogue, and soon the orders began rolling in.

Going against the dictates of the American Rose Society was heresy, and something of a feud developed between the Newark nursery and the society. It was resolved only after the ARS asked to borrow a color plate of a J. & P. floribunda for its yearbook. Perkins sent the plate, but with the provision that it could be used only if the society called the rose a floribunda. Press time for the yearbook was near, and the printer had left a blank space for the plate that had to be filled. An ARS official pleaded with Perkins to change his mind.

"Let us call it a large-flowered hybrid polyantha, Charlie."

"Nope. We call it a floribunda. If you're going to use our plate, you have to call it a floribunda, too."

And so, thanks to the problem of meeting the looming deadline, the picture ran with the floribunda designation, making it official. The controversy passed into history just in time for J. & P. to take advantage of the New York fair to promote Gene's favorite kind of rose.

World's Fair, Kordes' cross between Dance of Joy and Crimson Glory, was the hit of the garden. Forty thousand visitors left their names in the hope they'd be able to buy similar bushes for their homes. The names became the start of a mailing list that would expand to two million households, serving as the foundation for the nation's most successful mail-order nursery business.

Floribundas had been around for more than a generation of European gardeners, but the World's Fair display was their introduction to many Americans. Creation of the garden there ran into numerous difficulties. When the project was first discussed, the fair's promoters had promised to supply rich Long Island soil taken from a nearby potato farm. Instead, Boerner discovered to his dismay, the garden consisted of sub-soil dug up in excavating for fair buildings. It had no humus. It had only faint traces of the three essential fertilizing elements. It had been dumped on top of a former swamp.

Before the roses were planted, Gene ordered German peat moss to be mixed with the soil to give it a lighter texture, good aeration, and uniform acidity. Then four pounds of fertilizer were added for each hundred square feet. By the fall of 1938 the garden was ready for planting when a tropical storm swept northward and flooded the area with salt water. By the time the flood receded, the soil was in as poor condition for growing roses as it had been when Boerner first inspected the site. More peat had to be trucked in, more fertilizer added, but it was late in December before the last of the rose bushes had been planted.

Gene had always contended that fall planting of roses saved a year's growing time, a contention many gardeners disputed. Even so, the completion of planting on December 20 seemed to be carrying his theory a little too far. Before he left for his annual Christmas visit to Wisconsin, he left orders that the bushes should be kept uncovered until the last possible moment to soak up sun and encourage root growth. The temperatures were unusually warm for so late in the season.

It was still pleasant weather when he got to Wisconsin, but it was hard for him to keep his mind on the approaching holiday; he kept wondering what was happening to his rose bushes in Flushing. When Cedarburg's temperature suddenly dropped to below zero, he put in a hasty call to the United States Weather Bureau in Washington. The

Spartan, Floribunda (1955)

cold wave was heading toward Long Island, he was told. He telephoned a nurseryman friend near the fair grounds.

"Hill up those roses with peat moss. Pile on the salt hay. And don't wait until tomorrow — do it right now!"

The bushes were tucked into their protective covering before the New York temperature plummeted, and the following spring the bushes sprouted vigorously. To Boerner's satisfaction, those roses that had been planted in the fall did better than the ones that were added in March.

Things still not go smoothly at the World's Fair garden, however. The bushes planted in one corner languished. Investigation showed there was an underground gas leak there which had to be repaired before the roses would thrive. Then there was the problem with Japanese beetles. "We were knocking 'em off in pails," Charles Baldwin, who became traffic manager of the company, recalled some years later. "Each morning, we'd go through with a pail and brush and knock them off the leaves."

Such problems were eventually mastered, however, and Boerner was able to spend some time walking through the display, listening to people's comments. On one such afternoon he approached a middle-aged woman who seemed quite entranced by the roses, saying she wished she could have ones like that in her part of the country.

"Where are you from?"

"Oshkosh. You know, that's in Wisconsin."

Boerner told her he knew all there was to know about the climate there, and they chatted for a while before Gene moved on and approached a Vermont woman. "I'd just like to move this entire garden to my home," she told him. "But of course most roses just won't grow there."

A Long Island man told Boerner he'd tried to grow roses for years, but by the end of August the flowers and foliage were gone. Gene explained patiently to such pessimists that growing roses would be practical in their home climates if they'd take the trouble to learn how to do it. He described the problems with the soil at the World's Fair garden, the delay in getting the bushes in the ground. But with the proper feeding, spraying, watering, and soil mixture, the roses were doing well, as anyone could plainly see. With rare exceptions, any home in the United States was a suitable site for growing roses, he declared.

He understood, however, that many gardeners had neither the

knowledge nor the time to take such pains with a rosebush. His talks with passersby gave him valuable insight into why roses were not more widely grown in 1939 — the feeling, partly justified, that all but the old-fashioned June-bearing shrub roses were simply too much trouble. It was plain that hybrid roses must be developed that would stand summertime neglect and survive Wisconsin or Vermont winters.

Better varieties must be found, either by importing them from European hybridists or by hybridizing them himself, Boerner decided. He hoped that floribundas would be the answer for those who found the hybrid teas of that era too hard to grow, so he was interested to note the public reaction to them in the fair's garden. This was the first chance many of the visitors had been given to see floribundas. As far as he could tell, no one was disappointed. Boerner was there mostly to listen to the public's comments, but he also noted how the flowers themselves were doing in competition with each other. Joyous and Holstein were vigorous bloomers, Betty Prior grew taller than any of the other floribundas and, in general, the floribundas more than held their own with the neighboring beds of hybrid teas.

Thanks to the World's Fair display, Boerner assured Wilhelm Kordes, the royalty checks sent to him in Germany were certain to get larger. Kordes' royalties from J. & P. had amounted to a modest $201.24 in 1938, compared to $2,900.52 sent to Domenico Aicardi in Italy, but Gene told Kordes he hoped to sell thirty thousand bushes of Wilhelm's World's Fair floribunda the following season. "The garden will help us immensely to popularize the various new things," he assured the German hybridist.

The display was an oasis of natural beauty amid the hoopla and confusion of the fairgrounds, and visitors were numerous. Most came merely to look, but some asked attendants where they could buy bushes like these. At first they were told that the roses would be available at those nurseries which bought plants from the company for resale to home gardeners. But fairly early in the exposition it became plain to Charlie Perkins and Boerner that the garden's popularity opened up an intriguing possibility — a complete change in the company's method of marketing its product. Visitors to the garden were asked to leave their names and addresses. If the plants could be sold to them directly instead of through middlemen, it seemed obvious that Jackson & Perkins could keep a larger percentage of the profit.

A change in marketing methods was overdue. Selling roses to florists had not been easy during the Depression years, when getting food on the table was a problem in millions of American homes. It was all well and good for the Persian poet to advise that if a man had two loaves of bread, he should sell one and buy hyacinths. But when the man had to scheme and worry about raising the price of the bread, he had no heart for either poetry or flowers.

As the company's majority stockholder, Charlie Perkins had primary responsibility for keeping it afloat in a rising tide of deficits during the difficult thirties. At one point, J. & P. was $875,000 in debt, a far more worrisome sum then than it would have been some years later. By late 1938 Boerner was informing some of his European friends that Jackson & Perkins was "very seriously considering" going into the retail field. As he told Alex Dickson, Jr., the Irish nurseryman, the reason for this contemplated change was "to capture those potential customers which our dealers, through inertia or otherwise, are not always supplying with the roses which they are being asked for."

Perkins pointed out to Gene early in 1939 that the company's business had reached a plateau. The worst of the Depression was over, but neither sales nor profits were rising. To expand, it seemed plain, something new must be tried, and the roster of visitors to the garden gave the company a ready-made mailing list if it chose to go into the retail field. As a start, it was decided to sell rose bushes at the garden. The early results were only mildly encouraging. "Our retail selling has not been anything very heavy," Perkins reported to Boerner. "Sales are mostly small, but we figure that we are well advertised, even so." A heat wave in June of 1939 complicated things. The hot weather, Charlie wrote Gene, "knocked the garden silly." Still, the visitors' registration list continued growing, and it was decided to take the plunge into the mail-order business, while continuing to supply wholesale customers as before.

In 1939 the usual way of obtaining new roses was to get them from a neighbor — which meant, of course, that the roses were not very new, after all. But some of those who had visited the World's Fair garden sent back orders in response to the price lists J. & P. mailed to them, and by 1940 the company was selling about $80,000 worth of roses through its new retail department. Wholesaling accounted for the remainder of its $1 million gross that year. The figures were only mildly encouraging, but the company decided to persist with its retailing. This proved a wise decision. The time came when retail sales, conducted almost entirely by mail, accounted for two-thirds of Jackson & Perkins' revenue, helping to push its annual gross to twelve times the 1940 figure during the next quarter century.

Chapter VIII

Saving Europe's Roses

Besides helping with the World's Fair garden which changed the direction of his company's operations, Boerner spent part of the blooming season of 1939 in Europe on a buying trip. Such visits were usually routine breaks in his schedule, but this one took on a special urgency from the likelihood that war would soon cut off the United States from its European sources.

The Munich Pact had been signed the year before in a desperate attempt to appease Hitler and avoid a conflict which any sensible man dreaded. But by the time Gene sailed for Europe it was plain that such appeasement would not work. In March the Nazi troops had occupied much of Czechoslovakia. In April Mussolini's soldiers seized Albania. World War II did not begin until September 1, but it required no great ability as a prophet that summer to predict that it was coming.

Despite increased hybridization efforts at the Newark greenhouses, Jackson & Perkins still depended mostly on the Europeans to create new roses. Boerner wanted to rescue as many promising new varieties from German, French, British, and other growers as possible while the uneasy peace remained. In earlier European trips he had been satisfied if he found three or four hundred new roses to be tested and three or four varieties which survived the testing process and were found worth putting on the market. In 1939 he wanted everything he could get. He knew it might be a long time before he could go back for more.

The European growers were worried about the prospects of war but were still hopeful it would somehow be avoided. As far as their businesses were concerned, they were encouraged by the early results of the American patent law. It meant that their roses, imported for sale by United States firms, were protected and the royalties assured. But it was also obvious to them that with such profits possible from the creation of new rose varieties, the Americans would be tempted to bypass traditional European sources and hybridize the flowers themselves.

In England, Boerner found the weather wet and chilly, but the flowers were superb, he reported to Newark, and the fishing was excellent. At the Chelsea Rose Show he was appointed a judge of the novelty division, which gave him an early look at the new varieties. At Nottingham the eminent rosarian, Harry Wheatcroft, acted as his guide not only in the rose fields but through the cellars of a venerable inn.

Then it was off to Northern Ireland, where it was just as rainy and foggy as in England. He stopped first at the Samuel McGredy & Sons nursery, founded nearly a century before at Portadown near Belfast. The McGredys had been pioneer hybridizers of roses, their bushes famous not only for beauty but for hardiness. Gene approved of the original Sam McGredy's decision to use the Rugosa strain to encourage the hybrids to survive under difficult circumstances. Sam McGredy II had died, but Boerner found a kindred spirit in Walter Johnston, a brother-in-law who had taken over the hybridizing program. He was startled to hear the Johnstons' two young sons talking more like American teenagers than Irishmen. Their father explained that the boys spent most of their spare time watching American movies.

Boerner had met Sam McGredy II when the nurseryman visited the United States, remembering him as a dynamic sort of fellow who'd had high hopes for finding a market for Irish roses among all those Irishmen who had migrated to the New World. Now he paid his respects to Sam's widow and met their son, Sam III, who would one day carry on the family business. With Johnston he walked through the trial grounds where forty thousand bushes were being tested in the hope of finding four or five new roses that would be worth marketing.

From Portadown, Boerner went to Newtonards, where Dicksons of Ireland had been located since 1836. The combination of roses and rose history, encompassed in a single locality, was a heady one. Gene spent a night at the home of Alexander Dickson, Sr., and talked with him about the Dicksons' role in hybridizing. A stranger overhearing their conversation might have supposed they were gossiping. But when Gene pointed out that Lady Mary Fitzwilliam had been an enormously prolific old girl, adding much strength to the ancestoral line, he was speaking of an 1882 rose which the Dicksons had crossed freely with other varieties to produce their strains of hybrid teas. Such names as Dame Edith Helen, Edith Nellie Perkins, and Betty Uprichard came up in the conversation, too. But they were roses all.

The Dicksons claimed to have won even more gold medals than the McGredys. Many of their winners had been named for individuals — George Dickson, Col. Sharman Crawford, the Duchess of Sutherland,

Lord Lonsdale, and Mrs. Wemyss Quin. Gene thought that a rose named Mrs. Wemyss Quin might have done better with a pseudonym, at least in America, but he was polite enough not to mention it. Dickson described how a gold chain made from medals won by the family firm during the last one hundred years had been presented to the Newtonards Council to mark the firm's centenary. In the family house, Boerner was assigned a room overlooking meadows of brilliant green. The next morning the view was entirely hidden by fog; but when he walked downstairs, there were logs crackling in the fireplace and a cup of hot tea waiting.

Alex Dickson, Jr., showed him the test fields and spoke of his philosophy of hybridizing. His new rose, Dicksons Red, which J. & P. had introduced in the United States that year, was merely the forerunner of a new family of beauties, Gene told him. He noted that this rose was a darker shade — nearly black — in the Irish climate, while in America it was a vivid scarlet. Dickson's enthusiasm for roses in his test fields was tempered by worry over the threat of war. Boerner had noted when his plane arrived at Belfast that its landing pattern took it just above the Dickson fields. If bombers came to blast the airport, might the bombs not stray into these rows of roses? At any rate, he told Alex, he must have cuttings of every promising variety. If the worst happened, the roses would survive behind the impregnable barrier of the Atlantic.

After England and Northern Ireland, Boerner headed for Spain. He found that the recent civil war had "dislocated the rose fields and in some instances covered them with weeds," but Pedro Dot of Barcelona was preparing to plant the seedlings he had saved. Conditions were so unsettled in Spain that Boerner left for Italy after only two days. At the Aicardi nursery near San Remo he found the flowers were not at their best, except for Rome Glory and Signora, which were nearly shoulder high. He visited growers in Holland and Belgium, then went to France.

Paris seemed drab, he felt, but southern France was pleasant — the water of the Mediterranean bright blue, the house roofs red, the mountains gray. At Lyons there were rumors that France was about to mobilize to meet the German threat, but at an international gathering of rosarians there he met representatives of Germany as well as other countries. "The discussion took place over the bounteous board of the newlyweds, Mr. and Mrs. Francis Meilland," he wrote to Perkins in describing his Lyons visit, adding: "They were good eggs." On second thought, he crossed off this description to make it, "they are accomplished hosts," but added: "I must say, I didn't like being driven out of the kitchen where I rushed when I smelled the cooking." It rained all the time he was visiting the Meilland nurseries. It reminded him of a previous visit when he had walked through mud and pouring rain to see the garden at the Mallerin home in Varces.

In France, Gene also stopped to see Jean Gaujard, who had served an apprenticeship with Pernet-Ducher before taking over that great hybridizer's nursery in 1928. As Boerner was to note later, becoming the successor of the Frenchman known as "the world's greatest hybridizer" had put Gaujard in a difficult position, requiring him to live up to standards that were almost impossibly high. In Pernet-Ducher's declining years the nursery had lost some of its pre-eminence, and Gaujard's fellow rose growers in the Lyons area watched to see how the newcomer would fare. Boerner found Gaujard an "interesting, warmly aggressive man" who had modernized the selling end of his business. In fact, when the American arrived, he found a radio broadcast was taking place on the steps of Gaujard's office, the roses being promoted with the kind of enthusiasm reserved in America for selling soap. After the live broadcast had ended, Gene was asked to contribute to a recording made for future use on the air. He obliged, although he felt that having to stop at the end of each sentence so a translator could put his words into French rather cramped his oratorical style.

Once the broadcast was over, Gaujard introduced his visitor to Madame Gaujard and their two children, then took Boerner for a drive to a small restaurant along the Rhone. Gaujard was a connoisseur of good food, but Gene was no amateur at the table, either. The meal went well. On the way back to the nursery Gene was startled to hear a cannon shot. Had the war caught him here in southern France? But no, his host assured him. It was merely the official cannoneer who was shooting into threatening clouds to try to dissipate them and prevent hail from injuring the grapes before they could be picked. Boerner decided not to transport the custom to Newark. It would be nice to be able to control the weather over the rose fields, but the neighbors might object if there was an artillery barrage whenever hailstones threatened.

Back at the nursery Gaujard unlocked the stone-walled enclosure where Pernet had done his hybridizing. He showed Gene the cold frames where the seedlings were growing. Boerner particularly admired a rose called Ile de France, a warm pink suffused with yellow. It was among numerous varieties he arranged to take back to America, where its name was changed to Adoration. Another was Rose d'Or, which had added a hint of red to the pure yellow of the Souvenir de Claudius

Pernet. A third rose, which Gaujard called Lise Palais, was renamed Opal when J. & P. introduced it later on Boerner's recommendation.

The talk was not entirely of roses during Gene's visit to the valley of the Rhone. Gaujard was wondering what would happen to his business if he had to give up hybridizing for the Army. He had cause for concern. Mobilization came not long after Boerner left, and Gaujard's wife took over the nursery until France's defeat, when Gaujard was able to return home and raise roses again.

Boerner saved Germany for last. It pained him to see what the Nazis had done to what had been his favorite European country, but he looked forward to meeting such friends as Kordes and Tantau. When Kordes greeted him this time, there would be no need to worry about how they would recognize each other as there had been on Gene's first trip to Europe, when Wilhelm had written to say he would be in the station at Altona and Boerner would know him because he would be wearing a rose in his buttonhole. Not just any rose, Kordes added, but an appropriate one for greeting a visitor from the United States, a bloom of the variety called America.

By now, Kordes was calling Boerner "Uncle Eugene" and the two men had recognized they were kindred spirits. "Gene had a joyful heart and a boundless love for all plants," Kordes was to say some years later, and the combination suited the jovial German perfectly. The clouds of catastrophe were gathering, but the two men could ignore them for a while by concentrating on their mutual admiration for the rose.

Boerner checked into a hotel in Altona, an Elbe River port which had been annexed by the city of Hamburg only a year before. He was awakened the next morning by the sound of rolling drums and the peal of bugles.

"Well," he told himself, grimly, "it is here."

In every country he had seen numerous soldiers, but only in Germany had the troop trains kept rolling by, one after another. He climbed out of bed and went to the window. Below, a long line of conscripts was shuffling toward the railroad station. Many of the young men had girls or mothers hanging onto their arms. Some of the women were in tears. "It was saddening to me, knowing how the English were doing the same, day and night," he wrote to his sister in describing that morning. "I've no idea where it all can stop. Unless some crazy man starts something, there won't be war."

When he decided that the drums and bugles had not signaled the beginning of World War II, Boerner left his hotel and walked over to a drug store to buy post cards. He remarked to the druggist that it was sad to see the boys having to leave their families and sweethearts. "Sad?" the druggist said. "Forget it. We're getting ready for a lightning thrust that will teach the world and the damned Jews."

Boerner met Kordes at the Reichsgartenschau in Stuttgart. The German hybridist had driven there from Sparrieshoop with his niece and her young friend, an English girl named Mary Eaton. "We had jolly days together," Kordes said of that last meeting before he and Boerner were separated by the war. "It became a wonderful visit. Gene often recalled it."

Gene Boerner and Wilhelm Kordes examining some special roses.

The troubled times kept intruding, however. Kordes invited Boerner to attend a meeting of German rosarians. As they walked in, the other men stood up. Out shot their right arms in the Nazi salute. "Heil, Hitler!" they chorused. Kordes responded. Gene's arm stayed at his side

73

and he kept his silence. The room became absolutely still. Not until Kordes whispered to the chairman that his guest was an American and so should be excused from heiling der fuehrer did the tense atmosphere relax.

The Stuttgart show covered twenty acres, so Kordes and Boerner had much to see. Several deserted farms and old stone quarries had been transformed into a rose garden, with woods and small houses. It was a charming display, but the friends decided to leave a day early and motor along the Rhine, a trip which Gene later described as "two golden days of relaxation." They stopped at a restaurant opposite Godesberg, where the waiter escorted them to a table where Neville Chamberlain, the British prime minister, had dined while waiting his audience with Hitler to seek "peace in our time." "The sun was sinking in the west and the ruins on the other side of the Rhine, especially the so-called Rolandsboger, were lit as though they were on fire," Kordes said in describing that afternoon. "Nobody thought of war and all that was to follow in Europe."

As the trip continued, however, Boerner was reminded of the probability that this was no more than a final interlude of peace. When they reached the Autobahn, he dutifully admired this German engineering marvel and listened without comment to the claim that even the deer respected this highway and crossed only on the bridges provided, although he was sure that Wisconsin deer would never have behaved with such discipline. His sharp eyes noticed something else about the Autobahn — there was no telltale smear of oil drippings in the center of the lanes as there would have been on an American highway. He suspected that the Autobahn had not been built with private cars in mind.

In a letter to his sister he said he found some of the food in the German hotels ersatz, but the people were still managing to eat well enough at home. The countryside reminded him of the region around Cedarburg. The rural residents seemed to have been left to their own devices by the Nazis. "I spoke German right along with the natives, of course," he told Mrs. Schlueter, "but always said, 'good morning,' instead of 'heil Hitler' — but in English. I frequently got some awfully dirty, questioning looks." Boerner felt that Nazi propaganda was working mostly on the young. Unless the trend was reversed, he predicted, "the next generation of Germans will be a nasty one." The older people were "still imbued with the lovely old German philosophies" and couldn't believe the war was coming. "They actually remark with horror that the world is not thinking of another war," he wrote a little more than a month before Hitler sent his legions into Poland. "But the younger ones are goosestepping on to no one knows what."

If the war came, Europe would have little time for roses. The comfortable arrangement of relying on European sources for most of the new varieties for the American market would be ended. He had seen what the Spanish civil war had done to the nursery business in Barcelona, once one of Europe's principal sources of new roses. If the rest of Europe plunged into war, there would be an end to such luxuries as plant breeding. This would cause problems for Jackson & Perkins, he noted, but it would also offer opportunities. "America can become the new rose capital of the world," he declared.

As he traveled through eight countries, he felt it was up to him to rescue the inheritance of Europe's distinguished rose-growing tradition before the Nazi war machine began rolling across the fields. He lingered until late July before he boarded the Cunard White Star liner *Aquitania*, carrying ten thousand cuttings. Among them were the ancestors of varieties which would make him the world's leading rose hybridist. As soon as the *Aquitania* cleared port, Boerner sought out the captain. "I have a problem" he told him. "In those sacks I brought aboard are twelve hundred separate varieties of roses and a total of ten thousand cuttings from most of the countries of western Europe. Without your help, they will die."

A ship's captain is expected to be able to deal with a variety of problems, but this was a new one. However, these were unusual times and he was willing to cooperate. What, exactly, did Mr. Boerner want of him? "These cuttings must be kept refrigerated," Gene said. "And they can't be stored in a refrigerator with fruits and vegetables. Fruit and vegetables give off ethylene and that's bad for plants. They must be stored in the meat refrigerator." The captain was persuaded, the cooks were ordered to make room for rose cuttings among the roasts, and the *Aquitania* sailed westward with a horticultural legacy from the Old World, ensuring that when war came it would not interrupt the peaceful development of the rose.

Chapter IX

Finding Treasures In A Garden

According to the customary averages in rose hybridizing, only a few of the twelve hundred varieties Gene Boerner rescued from Europe could be expected to become marketable roses. But these were the best of the prewar European crop, so the odds were considerably better than usual. Among the varieties saved from wartime perils were such distinguished roses as Mrs. Miniver and Mandalay from France, Pinocchio and Garnette from Germany, Waves, Fantasia, and Grey Pearl from Northern Ireland.

The most significant booty from the standpoint of Boerner's future were the cuttings which became known as Pinocchio and Garnette. The latter had the uncommon quality of hanging onto its buds a week longer than most roses, a trait especially important in improving the strain of roses for the florist trade. As for Pinocchio, it not only became a most popular rose in its own right, but Boerner relied on it heavily in his development of the floribunda.

Garnette was Mathias Tantau's. Pinocchio's creator was Kordes.

Gene Boerner and Mrs. Frank Pearson are admiring some Garnette roses on his table at Gene's Landing.

Due to wartime shortages of labor and fuel, the German hybridists were forced to throw their test seedlings on bonfires a few months after Boerner's visit, so the buds the American took with him were soon the only stock of these roses remaining.

"It was more than great luck that the few buds Mathias sent came alive and well with Gene," Kordes said some years after the war. "Gene found out about the uncommon qualities of the Garnette. By the end of the war he could get it into greenhouses in quantity. It soon became the favorite of growers, sellers, and buyers.

"The same happened to my Rosenmarchen, renamed by him Pinocchio. This rose has on one side the Ophelia strain, which perhaps provides its heritage for early and generous response to greenhouse treatment.

"Well, Gene raised a wonderful range of small-flowered roses, and today eighty per cent of roses growing under glass for flower production are descendants of Garnette and Pinocchio. One of these Pinocchio children is his Masquerade. Rosenmarchen is not very fertile, but Masquerade sets seed like chickweed and the seeds germinate one hundred per cent. Everybody all over the world soon had Masquerade seedlings."

Pinocchio did not originally impress its creator, Kordes. "He thought I was crazy to bother with it," Boerner once remarked. "That was one time he was proved wrong, for we relied heavily on the Pinocchio for our development of the floribundas." When it was first tested in Newark, Pinocchio seemed hardly worth keeping. Its pink blossoms were smaller than the hybrid teas; and while Boerner had seen displays of floribundas in Germany, he wasn't yet sure that they would find a place in the American market. Still, Kordes' little bloomer was so vigorous and put forth its blossoms so enthusiastically that he hadn't the heart to discard it. "Eagerness in a rose is not only fetching but very desirable," Boerner said. "Such love of living nobody could deny and propagation was begun."

As early as 1941, Pinocchio had become a favorite of florists. Soon it was also available to home gardeners. Amateur rosarians who had found it difficult to grow hybrid teas decided this hardier floribunda was exactly what they were looking for and the orders came pouring in. "Pinocchio raised the status of floribundas to that of great roses," Boerner said.

Pinocchio, Garnette, and some of the other cuttings brought back from Europe in the *Aquitania's* meat refrigerator helped create a turning point in the rose business. The horticultural plunder from Europe was not only valuable in itself but provided research material for meeting the rose business's wartime challenge. The 1930 patent law had made domestic hybridizing potentially profitable. The loss of European sources of supply made it essential.

Along with a limited number of other American hybridists, Boerner plunged full speed into the breeding of roses, a painstaking process that he once said required all the skills of a surgeon. The first and most important portion of the process was cerebral, involving a decision as to which prospective parents offered the best chance of producing a worthwhile new rose. He had the records left behind by Dr. Nicolas, along with his own training and experience. Equally important, Boerner had the habit of regarding each rose as an entity with a distinct personality. One liked hot weather where another sulked when the temperature soared. Some varieties spent much of their energy producing vigorous bushes. Others were unusually capable of wintering successfully in a cold climate. Still another rose might be valuable mostly for its fragrance. There was no perfect rose. Perfection was the goal, but no hybridizer could expect to attain it. To come as close as possible to the ideal, Boerner set out to overcome one variety's weak points by crossing it with a type which had the qualities it lacked.

Pinocchio, for example, had the kind of family tree that made him believe it would be worth using in his hybridizing. One of its parents was Eva, a hybrid Muschata which Kordes had produced in 1933 from a cross between Robin Hood and J.C. Thornton. Pinocchio's other parent, also a Kordes creation, was Golden Rapture, a cross between Rapture and Julien Potin. Golden Rapture was a hybrid tea with large, double flowers, glossy foliage, and a clear golden yellow color. Eva was also a vigorous bloomer, with semi-double flowers of carmine red with white centers. Pinocchio's inherited vigor was exactly what Boerner sought in his attempt to make roses increasingly foolproof for amateur gardeners.

Some of Pinocchio's children in turn became parents of distinguished roses. Fashion, for example, was crossed with Geranium Red to produce Spartan, which came close to being Gene's all-time favorite, although, as a bachelor who considered his roses his children, he tried not to show undue partiality. These and countless other roses began as scribbles in Boerner's record book. Selecting the parents of a new rose was a process that combined scientific knowledge, practical experience, and sometimes a lucky hunch.

Finding Treasures In A Garden

Breeding a winning rose is even more complicated than breeding a likely candidate for the Kentucky Derby. Even for equine thorough-breds, genetics is far from a predictable science, but horses can be expected to resemble their parents to a considerable extent. Because all modern roses are descendants of long lines of hybrids, they do not come true from seed. A gardener who plants a particular variety of marigolds or petunias can look forward to flowers of a specified color and kind, but a rose hybridist who plants the seeds that grow in the rose hips after a flower is pollinated may wind up with almost anything.

The time may come when a hybridizer will discover how to fix the strain of hybrid roses, as wheat growers have done with hybrid wheat, making it possible to recreate the exact image of a rose from seed, a breakthrough which would not only reduce the time it takes to develop a rose but would prevent the deterioration of the strain that now takes place at the end of a rose's normal life span of ten to twenty years. Because of this ordained deterioration, each new rose now is doomed to be replaced within a quarter century, as has happened to such once-distinguished varieties as the American Beauty. As things stand now, however, a new rose can be multiplied only through budding or grafting. Thus a single rose bush is the direct ancestor of all others of its kind.

To complicate matters further, each rose is both male and female. It is capable of being a mother, a father or both, a versatility that need not be taken into account by horse breeders. Crimson Glory, for example, is the mother of Mardi Gras and the father of Detroiter. Poinsettia sup-plied the pollen for Mardi Gras, making it the papa, but it was the seed parent or mother of Detroiter. The resultant siblings were of divergent shades of red; their flowers were of different sizes, with one set of blossoms having thirty to thirty-five petals and the other only twenty to twenty-five. Their similar inheritance is not readily apparent to a casual passerby.

The hybridizing process is comparatively simple and anyone can do it with a little instruction. In fact, an amateur occasionally comes up with a cross which makes him a small fortune, although the odds against such luck are very high. A Cincinnati pipefitter, Carl Meyer, for example, spent his annual three-week vacations hybridizing roses, making two or three hundred crosses a year. In 1960, he crossed Pink Parfait with Pink Peace to produce a rose he called Portrait, the first bush hybridized by an amateur to win All-America honors. Early in Boerner's career as Jackson & Perkins' chief hybridist, he began to encourage such hobbyists to send him roses for testing. Most were worthless but a few paid off. A Canadian woman, for example, created a rose which proved profitable enough so she sent her daughter through college on the royalty checks.

Sometimes a valuable rose was discovered rather than hybridized. In 1934, for instance, a greenhouse proprietor in Richmond, Indiana, named J.H. Hill discovered such a sport and introduced it that Depression year under the optimistic title of Better Times. J.&P. was licensed to grow this new variety, which yielded as many as sixty handsome red blossoms per bush in a season. It did well enough in the garden, but it was an even more useful rose for greenhouse owners and florists. Before long more than half of the roses being sold for bouquets and corsages were Better Times blooms. Whenever a bush was sold, Joe Hill was entitled to a royalty. By the time his patent Number 23 expired, he had collected something like half a million dollars. As far as its originator's fortunes were concerned, the rose's name proved accurate.

Another example of how valuable a new variety could be was Blaze, for which J.& P. bought the rights from Joseph W. Kallay. The red climber, introduced in 1932, became one of the best sellers of all time. Before the Ohio nurseryman's patent ran out, Charles Perkins once observed, the company had paid him more than six hundred thousand dollars in royalties.

After Blaze entered the public domain, it continued to be so popular that Jackson & Perkins sought ways to cash in further on its reputation. The chance arose when Ralph Perkins, strolling in the garden behind his house in Newark, noticed that a Blaze bush had a single shoot that was still blooming profusely in mid-September. From that unusual shoot, an improved version of Blaze was developed and patented. Soon it was selling at the rate of nearly a million plants a year.

So it is possible to find a treasure growing in a rose garden, possible, though hardly likely. Most new roses come from carefully planned crosses. Boerner felt that part of the fun of gardening was trying to create a rose that had never been seen before, and he pointed out that the amateur could get into the hybridization lottery with such makeshift equipment as a pair of eyebrow tweezers, a small bottle of alcohol for sterilizing the equipment after each cross. and the kind of paintbrush that comes in a child's box of water colors.

"With the tweezers," he told a visitor to the Newark rose fields one afternoon, "you grasp the anthers of a full-blown rose and shake the pollen into a container. Then dip the brush into the pollen and delicately paint it onto the pistils of another variety of rose.

"That's all there is to it, except that afterward you tie a bag over the pollenized rose to keep the wind or bees from interfering with your work. About five months later, the seed pod will ripen. Remove the seeds and plant 'em and pretty soon you'll have seedlings of some brand new roses."

Even for a professional like Boerner, the odds were high against any one cross producing a winner; however, he felt there was no reason why a home gardener shouldn't have the thrill of creation that came from fathering a rose never seen before, even if the chances of it being worthy to compete in the marketplace were slim.

With hundreds of prospective parents to choose from, Gene selected the roses for the ten thousand crosses he made each season with considerable care, bearing in mind each variety's complex ancestral tree. Sometimes he was aiming for a particular color needed to fill out the spectrum in the company catalogue. Sometimes he was trying to get fewer thorns or longer stems or greater disease resistance or better fragrance. Invariably, he sought greater hardiness. When the subject came up, he was likely to mention his grandmother's Wisconsin farm and the memory of how often roses were winter-killed there when he was a boy. "I made a resolve to correct that some day," he said, "so the roughest climates could have as beautiful flowers as the more gentle ones."

As the inheritor of Nicolas' assignment to improve Jackson & Perkins' roses, Boerner joined a distinguished company of experimenters which went back to at least four centuries before Christ. According to the Roman historian, Herodotus, the hybridizers of 400 B.C. had managed to create a rose with sixty petals — twelve times the number of a wild rose's blossom. The ancients' progress was slow by modern standards, however. Five centuries later Pliny knew of only twelve varieties of cultivated roses. Now there are something like seven thousand.

Mrs. Nicolas turned over all of her husband's notes, horticultural papers, and books to Boerner to help him keep the research program going forward without a break after her husband's death. Jackson & Perkins was more active in trying to develop new roses than most companies of the 1930s, but it still depended largely on Europe. In its 1938 catalogue for wholesalers only one of the new roses listed had been created in the United States, a Nicolas floribunda called Smiles. Of the other seven, three had been hybridized in France, three in Northern Ireland, and one in Italy.

When the war cut off such traditional sources of supply, America found itself one of the few places where hybridizing could still be carried on. Boerner continued to keep up his contacts in Europe as much as possible; but even before the United States entered the conflict, commerce was difficult and mail unreliable. After Hitler's war machine began to occupy much of Europe, Gene's letters to Dutch hybridists were returned. Late in 1940 he got a final shipment of young plants from Kordes and Tantau by way of Italy, which was still neutral. But Kordes complained that "English bandits" had stolen his royalty check, and he suggested that future mail go by way of Japan and Russia.

Gene was delighted to hear that the medicinal value of the rose, once assumed to be a myth, was being upheld in wartime Britain. With citrus fruits scarce, the English remembered that rose hips are richer in vitamin C than oranges. Women and children gathered them by the ton so they could be processed for their juice.

Boerner was able to maintain sporadic contact with British growers. The McGredys and Dicksons converted most of their acreage to food production, but some hybridizing continued. In occupied France hybridizers continued to work, but they could no longer ship to the United States. As a result of the Europeans' troubles, American hybridizing made rapid progress during the war. As early as 1942, Boerner was predicting that there would soon be as many new roses produced in America as in all of Europe. "It will be a healthy thing for the rose lovers," he added. "With the greater competition, continuously higher standards will be set and the gardeners will benefit."

The rise of the American hybridists to world leadership had an important side benefit. Unlike any European country west of Russia, the United States had such a diverse climate that roses had to be produced which could thrive in regions as different as Wisconsin and Mississippi, Maine and New Mexico. Gene was convinced that the floribunda was particularly suitable for the role of a truly national flower; in fact, he did some lobbying among his Washington friends in a futile effort to have it recognized as such by Congress. What he called "the polyglot background" of the floribunda made it adaptable to widely-varying conditions of soil, temperature, and rainfall. In his crosses he sought to produce roses that would stand sub-zero northern winters and also thrive in the sub-tropical conditions of the southern tier of states. As his new varieties reached the market, he had proof of his success. Goldilocks, for instance, grew five feet in a single season in Florida and also flourished in chilly North Dakota.

Before many more years Boerner was able to report that the floribundas' breeding was "heading distinctly to disease resistance, hardiness, and a liberal inclusion of fragrance" with new colors and combinations of colors being added to the line. Hardiness with no sacrifice of beauty — that was the challenge. "It is up to the hybridizer to continue his work until he combines the two," he said, "and has the rose of the North with as much beauty as the rose of the more tender climates."

Boerner considered hybridizing "a field of romantic exploration," a chance to improve on Nature "by the cunning of man." "A hundred varieties have been created where one existed before," he wrote. "Just as in chemistry and medicine, however, the great discoveries do not inevitably result from research and design. Sometimes they are luck. They are stumbled upon. That is the romance of the game. That is the dramatic suspense. On any dewy morning, a miracle may occur... ."

Chapter X

A Rose For The General's Wife

The first seedlings from Boerner's hybridizing were in the fields at Newark during the summer of 1940. He was impatient for them to develop, for the company's entry into the retail field had increased the pressure to produce new varieties. In 1941, when an enlarged catalogue was distributed to the growing list of mail-order customers, sales had climbed by more than fifty per cent. Boerner predicted that by the spring of 1942 the mail-order business could easily amount to a quarter of a million dollars. "Of course, no one knows what the tightening up of general conditions is going to do to a business such as ours, which is rated nonessential," he wrote to an English friend. "It is difficult to get many of the things we need — paper, string, etc. They are all being absorbed by munitions production and the shipping of these products."

Writing to Charles Mallerin in France in the spring of 1941, he noted that sales were not only increasing to home gardeners but wholesale customers were also stepping up their rose orders. By the end of its second year in the retail business, he predicted, Jackson & Perkins would be selling as many roses as any of its rivals, and it soon hoped to surpass them. "We have been doing a lot of fundamental promotional work, such as sending out test plants to eighty-five different locations, joining in all flower shows and sending out a constant flow of publicity," he went on. "Our propaganda on floribundas has been phenomenally successful. In spite of the American Rose Society, the word, 'floribunda,' is now accepted."

Boerner took advantage of every opportunity to promote what he called "the new race of roses," recommending floribundas to gardeners who had previously been discouraged from trying roses because of climate. The flowers were not as large as those of the hybrid teas, he admitted, but "they are very freely produced under most trying conditions" and made colorful sprays of cut flowers available for the house nearly every day of summer.

By now Boerner's advice and comments were being sought by garden editors and others seeking simple but accurate information for amateur gardeners. He readily responded to such requests, which were one means of encouraging more people to grow roses. The advice he gave was certain to include several plugs for the floribundas, along with such suggestions as one he made to *New York Sun* readers to wear a rose to the office every day just because it would be "great fun and a most satisfying gesture."

Jackson & Perkins was rapidly growing into a big business, but much of the old informality remained. The offices were still in a converted white frame house on a Newark side street. The office cat wandered in and out. Charlie Perkins was being interviewed one afternoon by a *Collier's* writer when the cat started walking around on top of his desk with muddy feet. Perkins yelled for his secretary.

"You want me to throw out the cat, Charlie?" she asked.

"Oh, don't do that. Just put some newspaper on top of the letters so we don't get footprints all over them."

The display gardens were back of the makeshift office building. Visitors wandered through them. There were no fences. There were no signs telling people not to pick the roses, but none of them did. During the summer the twitter of strolling ladies in the garden mingled with the sound of birds.

About forty per cent of the company's Newark acreage had been converted to raising vegetables because of the war. This was not entirely voluntary. The government required thirty per cent of such land to be used for foodstuffs, but Perkins decided he could spare more in view of the shortage of skilled rose growers. Two-thirds of the company's land in California was also being used to raise food crops, with Mexicans brought north to harvest them. This acreage produced over three thousand tons of tomatoes, along with barley and other grains. At Newark the nursery's Victory Garden included a hundred acres of potatoes, fifty of carrots, fifty of beets, several hundred acres of grain, close to a hundred each of dry beans and peas. Fifty New York Chinese were hired to help the southern Blacks who had been employed, and Perkins hoped to get some Italian war prisoners, who were becoming plentiful now that the British were moving forward in North Africa. As it happened, the Italians never arrived, but later in the war the labor shortage was relieved by seventy-five German prisoners of war, who were held under guard in an abandoned schoolhouse when not working in the fields. Most of them considered this a pleasant way to wait out the war. Some managed to strike up friendships with the Newark girls.

Perkins and Boerner had joined other growers in establishing the annual All-America rose competition in 1940, with fourteen gardens designated that year as test grounds. Each grower sent his best new roses to the gardens, which were located in a variety of climates. The roses were watched by judges for a year or more. Scoring was based on vigor, disease resistance, and foliage as well as on the form, fragrance, and color of the flowers.

Before long, Boerner was having what he described as "a very severe argument with the American Rose Society" over the testing program. "Basically, what they are trying to do is to discourage the sending out of too many new varieties and have a much stronger pre-selection, with a heavier concentration on selling of the varieties which are good," he wrote to Alex Dickson. "Sometimes that works out very well, but sometimes there are varieties which are not good enough for a general distribution but may appeal to the specialists in some small areas of the country." Gene said he was considering adding a connoisseur's page to the company catalogue as an outlet for less-popular roses which some fanciers might want to try.

Early in 1941 patent number 437 was issued to a rose called Pan America, a cross between a Heinrich Wendland sport and a variety called Max Krause. Pan America had only a modest career, but it is significant in being the first of Boerner's patented roses, the forerunner of an unprecedented series of more than one-hundred-fifty patented varieties. A more important milestone was reached two years later, when a hybrid tea, the Katherine T. Marshall, became his first All-America Rose Selection (AARS) winner. This cross between Chieftain and an unnamed seedling was named for the wife of the wartime chief of staff, General George C. Marshall. The rose had pointed buds of a deep coral pink, suffused with yellow. When the buds opened, they were what Boerner described as a "warm, glowing pink," with a fruity fragrance. The stems were long, the foliage disease-resistant and, all in all, it was a rose in which its originator had taken considerable pride even before the results of the AARS voting were in.

Naming a rose for a well-known woman was common enough; Mme. Marie Curie and Mme. Chiang Kai-shek also had hybrid teas named for them that year. But for a few moments in the summer of 1942 Boerner wondered if he'd made a mistake when he decided to honor the general's wife.

Mrs. Marshall came to Newark to open a Jackson & Perkins promotional event called the Victory Harvest Garden Show and Gene

Pink-A-Boo, Floribunda (1961)

met her at the depot to drive her to the nursery grounds. After some small talk, he brought up the question: "How would you like to have one of my new roses named after you?"

Katherine Marshall gave no sign she had heard. She kept gazing thoughtfully out of the car window. Boerner began to feel uneasy. Had he violated the proper protocol in dealing with generals' wives? Could it be that the wife of the nation's top military man was offended at the suggestion? Perhaps she felt that her name should not be used in what was, after all, a commercial venture. The silence continued for several minutes. Finally, Gene said he was sorry he had brought the subject up. "I hope I haven't hurt your feelings, Mrs. Marshall."

Her reverie ended, she turned to him, smiling, and assured him her feelings were unbruised. It was just that his offer had reminded her of her girlhood, she said. "I grew up on a farm and one day my father told me: 'Katie, the next time the cow has a calf, I'll name it after you.' I was thrilled. I kept waiting and waiting. Finally, sure enough, there was a new calf in the barn."

"And your dad named it Katherine?"

"He couldn't. It was a bull. He couldn't have a bull around the farm named Katie. So I missed my chance then. Now it seems I'm to have another. You can see why I'm delighted to have your rose named after me."

Having the blessings of the general's wife for the rose was a triumph. During the war there was an undercurrent of worry around Newark that gardeners would regard only vegetables as suitably patriotic. In general, however, Gene considered the business omens favorable. All those Victory Gardeners were getting the habit of digging in the earth and watching things grow. Many of them could be expected to continue the hobby after peace returned. They would offer a fine new market for Jackson & Perkins' roses and perennials.

Defense plant workers were bringing home bigger pay checks than most of them had ever received before. The migration to the suburbs was beginning, despite gasoline rationing. The company's mailing list kept growing. Boerner assured these new customers that they could plant roses with a clear conscience because England, which had been in the war longer, was encouraging its citizens "to preserve and continue its floriculture for morale purposes."

Jackson & Perkins began to publish a "Rose Letter and Plant Research Review," mostly written by Boerner. It was sent to editors in the hope of a plug. It also went to horticulturists and leading rose-growers. Along with advice on rose-growing and information about new varieties, Gene managed to get in a few general comments about how "the Queen Anne's lace is giving way to the goldenrod" or descriptions of the way "the first trees are flaming on the highest dry spots in the hills." The "Rose Letter" urged Victory Gardeners not to be carried away with their vegetables to the point where they failed to plant flowers and shrubs. Boerner pointed out that an official of the federal public health service had said the soldiers would fight vigorously for their country "if they remember it is a place of lovely lawns and fragrant blossoms." He quoted with approval a statement by Dr. Liberty Hyde Bailey, an eighty-four-year-old professor emeritus at Cornell: "When troubles convulse the world, there is inspiration and comfort in a rose."

Boerner modestly stopped short of urging that all those comforting roses be purchased from J. & P., but he did place considerable emphasis on the merits of the floribundas that the company was now promoting so heavily. A bed of World's Fair floribundas had survived two winters in the Berkshires, he reported. Betty Prior bushes left uncovered at twenty below had lost only the tops of their branches.

He predicted that after the war Americans would follow the fashion he had observed on his European visits of 1937 and 1938, when he had seen as many as ten thousand floribundas in a single planting. Meanwhile, he advised putting floribundas around every house, perhaps setting them off with evergreens. Too many Americans had gone too far from their gardening heritage, he declared, and now was their chance to return to the soil.

"In spring, as the frost leaves the ground and the first smell of the warm earth reaches upward, the inherent urge to plant something that will grow grips the country. Now is the opportunity to indulge this urge to its fullest. With the limiting of tires and gas, with the elimination of golf balls and other play equipment, the home becomes once again the focal point of the American family ...."

"From a purely selfish point of view, the health and renewed spirits gained from gardening are beyond measure to the individual indulging in it. The joy of sharing both the beautiful yards and the resultant cut flowers with initimates and passersby and the morale-building effect of it all are going to be cherished during the years of war ahead of us and will renew our heritage in the soil."

The need to persuade reluctant gardeners that the soldiers' morale depended on floribundas as well as mom and apple pie was only one of the wartime problems. J. & P. had planned to bring out Fantasia, an import from Ireland, in 1943, for example, but the skilled help was mostly in service or war plants by now and what Boerner described in an apologetic letter to Alex Dickson as "a mishap in our budding fields" cut production of this rose to the point where its debut was postponed. Two other Dickson roses, Prima Donna and Waves, were introduced that year, however. The latter had not done very well in the AARS competition, Gene told Dickson, but "we named it in honor of the women members of our Navy and hope we may be able to build up a sale in that way."

The year before, J. & P. had introduced one of Nicolas' creations, named for a popular radio personality, Mary Margaret McBride, and by 1943 the intermingling of rose business and show business became more complete. Metro-Goldwyn-Mayer initiated the friendship. Early in the war the movie company had decided to make a tear-jerker about the plucky British, hiring a charming young woman named Greer Garson to play the title role, "Mrs. Miniver." The script called for the town stationmaster to win a prize for a red rose he had developed, and, gallant fellow that he was, he named it for his lovely neighbor.

MGM wanted a new rose which could not only play its role in the movie but would be named after Mrs. Miniver in real life. The movie would promote the rose, and the rose would promote the movie. Boerner chose a French import, Souvenir de Louis Simon, renaming it Mrs. Miniver for the English-speaking world, and both movie and rose did well in the marketplace. As for Miss Garson, she captured the hearts of both casual movie fans and the jury of her peers, who awarded her an Oscar. Gene chose another French import, renamed it the Greer Garson, and made sure that a handsome bouquet of these flowers was presented to their namesake when she walked on stage to receive her award.

The profitable collaboration among MGM, Miss Garson, and Jackson & Perkins did not end there. When the actress moved on to break box-office records in her next role, Mme. Marie Curie, a yellow rose from France was renamed in honor of the woman scientist — and of the uses of Hollywood publicity.

Chapter XI

Picking Up The Pieces

With his two favorite assistants in the Army, Boerner worked long hours during the war years, with little time for relaxation. He missed those annual jaunts to Europe, the chance to stroll through the rose fields and talk about the mysteries of hybridizing with Germans and Frenchmen, Irish and Englishmen, Dutchmen and Danes.

In April of 1945, just as things were busiest in the nursery, he was forced to lie in a hospital bed, fretting over the wasted time, while the doctors built back his strength. Later in the year, pains in his back convinced him that he had arthritis, but an X-ray indicated his trouble came from a ruptured spinal disc. Dr. S.A. Munford told him he could either wear a brace for an indefinite period or have an operation. He chose the operation as the lesser evil and checked into St. Luke's Hospital in Chicago, where the offending disc was removed. He spent Christmas there, the first time in many years when he had not gone home to Wisconsin for the holiday.

He hoped to be back on the job within three weeks, but by the end of February in 1946 he was still able to work only three hours a day. Still, he began making plans to go to Europe. With the war over, he was anxious to see what had happened to his friends, not to mention their roses.

But civilian travel was difficult to arrange. Postwar shortages of food, fuel, and clothing in Europe made it necessary to discourage any unnecessary visits to that troubled continent. Meanwhile, the first letters Boerner had received from some of the European hybridists since early in the war began arriving. He was especially glad to hear from Kordes. Wilhelm had tried to carry on, sowing rose seeds as usual in his greenhouse benches. But with no coal to heat the buildings, the seeds did not sprout. Stubbornly, he sowed another crop. The next winter, fuel was obtained, the greenhouse was heated, and the following spring Kordes found he had two years' crop of seeds, all sprouting at once.

Mrs. Marguerite de Noyeal, whose nursery had originated the roses Boerner had named for Mrs. Miniver and Greer Garson, reported her house had been burned in 1944 by American bombers. There had been numerous restrictions on her work during the German occupation, she told Gene, but she had kept her rose seeds and planned to resume hybridizing.

The postwar shortages in Europe gave Boerner new chores to do in supplying his fellow hybridists. Alex Dickson wrote that he hadn't tasted ham in six years, and Boerner promptly sent him some, along with other foodstuffs that were still scarce in Britain. He supplied one of the Dutch hybridists with shoes for his children and coffee and tobacco for himself. Kordes wrote of his joy at getting a parcel from Boerner containing real wool. His wife was nearly overcome. "It is years since she had such soft wool in her hands. For the first time in the twenty-six years I'm married, my old woman said that roses were a good job after all. The man who planted his land with these useless brambles has risen in her consideration, too."

The flood of East German refugees had been given what supplies could be spared, Kordes said, but "now we are all at the end of our wits." He noted that a newspaper statistician had figured out that at the current production rate, each German would be able to get one overcoat every ninety-eight years. The war stopped almost on his doorstep, Kordes reported, and left the buildings intact, but he had been digging stumps in the forests to cook food and keep warm.

Rose-growing had been cut to just a fraction of what it had once been, Kordes' letter went on. His son had been crippled in the war. A nephew was still a prisoner in Russia. All Kordes could do at the moment was try to grow vegetables for his hungry neighbors. He would be grateful for coffee, tea, fats of any kind. He would also like the *American Rose Annual* and the new edition of *Modern Roses*. If Eugene came for a visit, he warned, he should bring his own food and arrange for a permit to stay in Kordes' house as the hotels in Hamburg were in ruins. The library of the Verein Deutscher Rosenfreunde at Sangerhausen, with its detailed records of all the work of German hybridizers, had been taken to Russia, Kordes reported.

Despite the war, he had introduced a scarlet floribunda, Sondermeldung, which won the Bagatelle gold medal in France in 1943. It was one of the hardiest roses in his fields, he added. Perhaps when commerce could be resumed, Uncle Eugene would be interested in Sondermeldung? Boerner was interested, all right, but not in marketing a rose with a name so hard for Americans to pronounce. When the floribunda was introduced some years later, he renamed it Independence.

From Italy, Aicardi reported that his estate at San Remo had been ruined by the Germans. Many of the plants which survived the Nazis had been killed by another pest, an infestation of grubs. The Partisans had then arrived and relieved him of half a million lire and other valuables. San Remo had been hit a hundred times by air and naval bombardments, he reported. The town's flower market had been blown to bits. "I have to start again," the Italian hybridist said. "I have saved something and I have great hope, but I am financially ruined, for my savings and rents are nearly worthless. The wages of a land workman is over four hundred lire a day instead of the previous twenty. Nobody is willing to work, preferring to bother in odd commerces." Boerner added Aicardi to his list of those who were receiving packages regularly, and the Italian wrote back to say that when he got Gene's letter saying such help was on the way, "I burst into tears."

Jean Gaujard reported that during the five years since the war began, he had managed to continue his hybridizing, even though most of his nursery had been converted to vegetable production. "Now France is free at last," he wrote. "We have seen the American Army here. Several tanks were near my office, and a cannoneer of a tank was from Newark." One of Gaujard's roses, Condrieu, which had been renamed the Mme. Marie Curie, had been picked as an All-America winner. Boerner passed along the good news to its originator.

Jackson & Perkins had missed out on an even more successful French import, a hybrid tea developed by Francis Meilland. The Frenchman named it Mme. A. Meilland, after his mother, but it became famous under the less-unwieldy title of Peace. J.&.P. got first crack at the American rights and turned them down, a decision that Charlie Perkins had to keep explaining over and over again in the years to come. One story was that Perkins had predicted Peace would never catch on, but this was not the case. Boerner and Perkins liked the rose, but Charlie did not like Meilland's demand for a thirty-three per cent royalty instead of the usual fifteen. Perkins was willing to go to twenty, but no higher. As a result, the Conard-Pyle nursery introduced the rose. Peace was a particularly welcome word in 1945, and the name and shrewd promotional work helped create an unprecedented demand for the rose. But its 9.6 rating by the American Rose Society — a record high score at the time — indicated that the plant itself was mainly responsible for its own success.

Picking Up The Pieces

Gene spent much of the summer of 1946 trying to arrange to go to Europe. Some of the growers there were shipping buds to Newark again, but much of the rosewood arrived in poor condition because of the delays en route. Boerner urged such hybridists as Gaujard to come to the United States so they could discuss the rapidly-changing American rose market face to face.

The postwar red tape was finally unraveled, and Boerner flew to London on August 20, going from there to Holland and France. He was unable to get permission to visit Aicardi in Italy. Even more disappointing, he was unsuccessful in obtaining the special permit needed to visit Kordes and Tantau in occupied Germany. In Washington, before he left, he had tried to persuade the authorities to give him the permit as an American businessman. When he was turned down, he argued that he should be allowed to visit Sparrieshoop in the sacred name of science. But this argument was also unavailing.

In the Boskoop area of Holland, he found the nursery stock almost intact. "The Germans had been planning to use this material to re-beautify Europe and had not destroyed it," he noted. "In fact, they had purchased material from some of the nurseries throughout the war."

The Dutch told him that Tantau in Germany had survived and was starting to hybridize again. After stopping in Belgium, he went to France and renewed his friendship with the "temperamental, tempestuous and artistic" Mallerins, who, he said, had some lovely things. Back in England, he spent a day with Courtney Page and other friends. The Haywards Heath testing grounds was fairly denuded, but the English were making an effort to restore it. In Northern Ireland, McGredy and Dickson were hybridizing roses again but had little ready to show just yet. He had found a few interesting roses but hardly enough to make the trip worthwhile. He still had not completely recovered his health, and he cut the journey short, returning home convinced that obtaining much usable material from Europe would have to await further progress in the postwar recovery.

By December he was still weary from the trip, but he didn't intend to miss two Wisconsin Christmases in a row. When he got there, he claimed in a letter to the Harrisburg rosarian, J. Horace McFarland, "I slept for four days without a break."

The occupation authorities had kept him from visiting Kordes, but the mails were going through with some regularity now and Boerner was able to tell Kordes that while he'd been cut off from news of the American rose market his Pinocchio had become one of the largest-selling roses in the United States. German funds were still frozen, but Gene told him to be patient. The red tape would be cut through one of these days, and meanwhile his royalties were accumulating. Kordes wrote back that he feared a Communist takeover of West Germany. If he were faced with deportation to Russia, he added, he had enough poison on hand to secure burial in his beloved Holstein.

But the Russians stayed away, and, as conditions inched back toward normal, the German hybridist found he would be allowed to import budwood from America. He was anxious to obtain new varieties as the first postwar "reinforcement of the old guard," he said in dispatching an order to Jackson & Perkins. Apparently he omitted the word "not" in listing which varieties to send; and when the package arrived, it contained not only new roses but numerous old varieties which he had in plentiful supply. This set off a flurry of trans-Atlantic correspondence, with Gene explaining that he had thought it odd that Wilhelm wanted such old standbys as Better Times, but that he had sent them on the theory that something must have happened to wipe out all Kordes' nursery stock.

It was not until 1948, nine years after they had last met, when Boerner and Kordes were finally able to get together. In celebration Wilhelm took Gene for a drive through a portion of Holstein where some of the American's ancestors had lived. "Some day," Boerner wrote to a friend, "I'll check to see if they were honest burghers or plain horse thieves. I'm still inclined toward the first." His ancestral region of Germany, he noted, varied from rich farm land to acreage "good only for Christmas trees." The jaunt ended at a rathskeller where "the food was delicious — oxtail soup, tenderloin steak, french fried potatoes, cauliflower, a cheese and coffee dessert." Kordes was driving "one of those tiny cars that make you put your knees under your chin if you want to be comfortable," but it sped along at a comfortable forty miles per hour.

Boerner found everything in Germany "sad and dilapidated looking." In Hamburg, he sat up all night talking with some of his prewar friends. "When they complained too much, I told them: 'After all, you lost the war.' And then I preached democracy and tried to explain it and how it works." His Hamburg friends couldn't understand why their city had been bombed. Boerner pointed out that London had been bombed first.

Cars were not supposed to be driven on Sunday without a special permit. When he and several of the Germans tried it, they got a ticket from a policeman, who came wheeling up on his bicycle. Then it was off to lunch in the same house where he'd dined in 1939, eating some of the food that Boerner had sent ahead. "Again we talked democracy and here I demonstrated freedom from fear. The other time, the host had jumped up three or four times to see if anyone was listening at the doors, but he didn't have to do it this time."

In Italy, Aicardi met him at the San Remo station with effusive thanks for the postwar parcels, then took him home where "his mustached brother" and the women of the family thanked him, too.

In France, Boerner felt that Gaujard was "hybridizing in a circle" by concentrating too much on a single strain. He predicted that the Italians would soon surpass the French as rose breeders. As for Kordes and Tantau, they were doing fine work. "The future of hybrid tea shaped flowers really lies here," he said. He was surprised to notice that Pinocchio did not seem very vigorous in Germany, but put it down to the vagaries of the rose world.

At Dickson's in Northern Ireland he had a restful time as a houseguest, the family providing him with a big chair, scotch, a hot bath, a hot water bottle, and even bacon and eggs for breakfast. He noted that the English and Irish hybridists had been hard hit by the war, but he decided the curtailment was not all bad: "I saw less overgrown, space-consuming stock and far more healthy, vigorous young stock in a better assortment of varieties.

"The American standards of improved bushes as well as improved blooms have left their impression on the whole world," he reported in evaluating his trip. "I think all rosedom will gain by it. As the hybridists gain control of the plant, they will concentrate even more on the flowers and these, too, will show the effects of the new trends in the rose world." The European test gardens were slowly regaining their prewar status, he added. But the residents of that part of the globe still were finding it "difficult to concentrate on flowers when flour is still scarce."

Chapter XII

Papa's Roses

Back home in Newark, Boerner was more than ever convinced that the United States had become the center of rose hybridizing. The time would come when Europe would again be important in the field, but he felt there was no reason why it should be allowed to recapture its old pre-eminence. The market for fine roses was growing rapidly. The opportunities were expanding. Both as a matter of personal pride and as a matter of good business, it was important that Jackson & Perkins lead the way in improving its principal product.

Each morning after breakfast Gene walked past the benches where the results of his crosses were growing, taking notes. It was he who decided which roses should be crossed, although the actual chore of transferring the pollen from one plant to another might be performed by a trusted aide. A good garden rose was seldom a good florist's rose, and he had to try to create outstanding examples of both. A greenhouse rose was most valuable if it bloomed in January, when the days were short, but even under artificial conditions many garden roses "came blind" in the winter when cut flowers brought a premium price.

On the average it took four years before a decision could be made on whether a promising rose was worth keeping. Those roses which were nearly but not quite good enough were the ones Boerner found it hard to discard. Sometimes there were arguments with Charlie Perkins or others, for men can differ on which rose is most likely to find a market. Sometimes there were roses which were lovely enough to compete, but too nearly like an established variety to be worth promoting. Sometimes a rose might lose out simply because there was a limit on how many new ones could be introduced into the catalogue in a given year.

Perhaps twenty per cent of the seedlings survived the first winnowing process and were moved from small pots into beds. About a fifth of these survivors were eventually budded in larger quantities to be given a further look. And so the attrition went on, with the standards raised successively higher as the final moment of decision — to market or to discard — approached.

Papa's Roses

Boerner judged the roses on a long list of attributes — color, foliage, flower production, stem stiffness, fragrance, ease of growing, degree of immunity from disease, among others. The European imports ran the same gauntlet as Boerner's hybrids but were kept in a separate section and given a different code of numbers.

Gene came to think of individual roses as having distinctive personalities. Some hung their heads — out with them. Some of the reds had a tendency to blue as the petals faded — out with them. Some were finicky about temperature, thriving in the cool and humid days of late spring but languishing when temperatures climbed. So out with them, too, unless they could be useful as roses for the greenhouse, where temperatures could be controlled.

Some roses, like some people, had a special dislike for winter. In the hothouse, tended with science and skill, they put out only a useless blind shoot in December. But Gene knew that a lot of good roses behaved that way and that the ones which looked least promising when the snow lay thick on the ground might prove to be the most vigorous of the lot the following June.

Scurrying around the Newark acreage, full of plans and projects, Boerner was inclined to raise his voice and shout when frustration loomed. But, for the most part, his associates liked this big, hearty man with the big, hearty voice. There were those who dared to yell right back, which seemed to be all right with him. During harvest time Gene was apt to arrive at his office bearing baskets of ripe tomatoes or boxes of grapes, handing out this largesse to family men at the nursery to make sure all this good food would not be wasted.

His duties often involved taking important visitors around the premises. Greenhouse operators might arrive in a group, and he would palaver with them in their specialized jargon as they made the rounds, studying a promising rose here, poking into a humid hothouse there. If the visitors were women — a delegation from a garden club, perhaps, in pastel dresses and floppy hats — Boerner was the Old World gentleman, strolling through the gardens to point out the roses like a father showing off his children, making sure to make special mention of those that were his favorites. Garnette was one of these. Tantau had produced this profusely-blooming floribunda which was a favorite of florists but valuable as a garden rose as well. Boerner was convinced that it was a superior rose for breeding purposes — "he worked that strain into everything," one associate said, exaggerating only somewhat. Later, there were other favorites — Spartan, most notably, and Fashion.

Along with his other duties, Boerner was now the company's prize promotion asset. He loved to talk to anyone who admired roses. He was able to speak of scientific matters in laymen's language, which made him a favorite of visitors whose enthusiasm about roses exceeded their knowledge. He had firm feelings about what sorts of roses were worth growing. At one flower show, several women judges were enthusiastic about a rose whose center was what Boerner called "crumpled up." He disagreed with them. "You wouldn't buy a thing like that," he told them.

"No," one woman said, exercising her right to the last word, "because you wouldn't let it into the flower shops."

Boerner was a gregarious man who welcomed company even when he was trying to work out plans for the business or decide one of the problems associated with rose-breeding. "When he'd come into the greenhouse, he'd give a yell and I'd go over," one colleague testified. "He needed to have somebody to talk to while he was thinking."

Those who worked with him were convinced that his knack with roses was something more than science. "It was a gift he had," one of them said, years later, looking back on those days. "Many of the fellows who'd learned plant breeding in college would say he was off his rocker because he was ignoring the rules. But he could sense quality in a rose, inbred quality. Gene would keep crossing and recrossing to get the characteristics he wanted. By the end of six years, he'd have at least three original crosses plus a recross and a third cross."

Like any home gardener, Gene returned to look at certain pet roses again and again. Charlie Perkins had his favorites, too. The company president liked to get away from his office to walk past the rows of blooming bushes. Other members of the firm were seldom far from the nursery end of the enterprise, either. Ralph Perkins, for example, developed a particular fondness for a rose called Revelry. It was tried as a greenhouse forcing variety, but, alas, it never caught on. Gene enjoyed pointing out Revelry to visitors. "That's Ralph's rose," he would say, slyly. At lunch, sitting around with the others in what was more like a family gathering than a business session, Ralph had to put up with remarks about his mistaken loyalty to what was soon a discontinued rose.

Many of those who worked for Jackson & Perkins had started as boys, gradually rising to greater responsibility as they grew older. The business was expanding rapidly now that it had joined the retail field. In 1930 it had managed with only five greenhouses. Two more were added before World War II shortages put a stop to construction. As soon as materials became available, three more were erected. With ten green-houses capable of handling fifty thousand plants each, it seemed the nursery was big enough. But as sales soared, more buildings were added, until the number of Newark greenhouses finally reached twenty-seven.

With the expansion came new responsibilities for Boerner. He worked long and hard and expected others to do the same. When he was trying to get something done, he could lose his patience when someone erred, and was willing to show his displeasure at the top of his voice. "He was hard and he had to be hard," one of the old employees said of Boerner's activities in those days, "but his heart was gold. If he had to tell you something, he didn't pull punches; but if he was wrong, he admitted it. He knew his business. Nobody put something over on him."

At Jackson & Perkins, the year began each July 1 and ended June 30, with a bonus given to the employees depending on how the business had prospered. An individual's bonus varied with how well he had performed his job during the fiscal year. Some of those Gene yelled at most consistently learned later that he'd gone to bat for them at bonus time, urging that they get a liberal share of the kitty.

Gene studying some of his plantings in the rose fields at Jackson & Perkins.

By now, the research program at Newark occupied five large greenhouses, two test gardens, and thirty-five acres of field trial grounds. Assisting Boerner was a large staff there and at Newman, California, where the experimental gardens covered one hundred acres.

Successful pollination was only the first step in trying to develop a new rose that would be good enough to market. After about six months the cross resulted in a few seeds which could be planted in flats where, if all went well, they sent up small shoots. A month or two later, after two or three true leaves formed, the seedlings were transplanted to small pots. Beginning in mid-April, such seedlings could be set out in the field after the first flower had faded. This early bloom seldom gave more than a faint indication of a rose's prospects, even to such a practiced eye as Boerner's.

By the end of the first autumn a few selections were made and budded on rootstock. But most decisions on whether a rose was worth keeping were postponed until the plant's second year in the field. During this second year and possibly a third the roses were watched with experienced skepticism, leavened with hope. The odds were twenty-five hundred to one against any particular cross producing a winner, and Gene eliminated the weaker candidates with necessary ruthlessness. Some of the roses were obviously not worth keeping, but others showed just enough promise to be tested further. The elimination process eventually resulted in a few survivors which Boerner believed were worth propagating in larger numbers and sending to the company's trial gardeners throughout the country for testing in a variety of climates. Of ten thousand crosses perhaps a dozen or two had survived the sifting and winnowing that preceded this next-to-final step. Then it was only if a one-sided majority of the test gardeners praised a rose that it was decided to propagate it by the tens of thousands and include it in future catalogues.

With thousands of roses being hybridized each year, the process followed a carefully-planned routine. During most of his years as a hybridizer Boerner depended on such trusted assistants as Mrs. Margaret Pullen, who worked for the company for seventeen years.

"We'd get to the greenhouse at 7 a.m. and see if the plants needed water," Mrs. Pullen said. "The roses which had been potted in February would start blooming in May, so that's when the hybridizing began. We'd take the cans of pollen collected the day before — the pollen was kept in little cans like the ones salve comes in, with a paper cap you could write the numbers on — and we'd make as many as five hundred crosses in one morning. Then we'd clean the pollen from other roses, picking it off with tweezers and putting it into those little cans, always keeping track of each variety by writing down its number.

"After it dried the pollen could be brushed on another rose. Then we'd put on a metal tag to keep track of the cross. In the greenhouse, where there wasn't any wind, we didn't have to cover the crosses. If it was done outdoors, we'd cover them with cellophane bags. By the end of July, when the pollinating was done, we would have made anywhere from ten to fifteen thousand crosses.

"I might be the one who actually made the cross, but it was Mr. Gene who told me what crosses he wanted to make. We'd go through the greenhouse together and he'd say, 'I want to cross this one with number so-and-so.' He never had to look up a number. He kept it in his head.

"He always made each cross for a reason. For instance, there might be a variety with a beautiful blossom but a poor plant. He'd cross it with a rose with a single blossom but a good plant. Or he'd cross a rose with a weak stem with one that had a strong stem.

"Every year when we started the hybridizing, one thing Mr. Gene wanted to do was make a blue rose. If we got a red with a little bluish cast he'd use it on everything in the hope he'd get a truer blue. He'd cross a lavender with red to get a deeper lavender or deeper red. One year he got one that turned blue as it started to fade. He thought the blue might carry through on some other crosses, but it didn't.

"In the fall, after the seeds got ripe, we'd pick them and put them in bags and plant them in flats. Each variety got a number at that point. You might get fifteen seedlings with the same number, even though the seedlings from the same seed pod wouldn't be identical.

"When they'd get big enough, we'd bud them on Better Times or some other strong variety in the greenhouse. When we'd get eight or ten eyes, we'd send them to California to be budded onto rootstock in the field. They'd grow ten or fifteen to test in the field, then bring them back, and plant them in the greenhouse in Newark. We'd watch to see if they were greenhouse roses or would prove themselves outdoors. We'd ship some of them to Europe, and the hybridizers there would pick the ones they wanted, just like we'd test the ones the European hybridizers sent here."

Operating on such a large scale, J. & P. had to have ten to fifty thousand bushes on hand of any variety listed in its catalogue. Each of those bushes traced its ancestry to a single tiny seedling. "From one plant the first year," Mrs. Pullen explained, "you might get five eyes. Each eye would be budded and produce one plant. So now you have five plants. From those, you could get five or ten eyes from each, which means at the end of that generation you have twenty-five to fifty plants.

From those you'd get one hundred fifty to three hundred, and they would produce enough eyes so you'd get a thousand to fifteen hundred plants. And so on. It was a long process, you can see. That's why it would take at least five years before a new rose went on the market, and usually more.

"When a rose looked good in the A greenhouse, we'd put fifty to a hundred bushes in the B greenhouse, which was where the growers came to look at the new varieties. Mr. Gene would listen to the growers' comments, but he wouldn't always agree with them. Sometimes the growers didn't like a rose but he did. I can't remember once when they were right and he was wrong. Take Woburn Abbey, for instance. It had mildewed in the greenhouse, and the growers didn't think much of it. But he liked it anyway, and it turned out he was right."

Mrs. Pullen and other women who worked in the hybridizing program called Boerner "Mr. Gene" to his face; but when they thought he wasn't listening, they were sometimes more flippant. One morning he overhead them talking about "Papa's roses." The next day he called Mrs. Pullen into his office after she'd made her rounds of the greenhouse. "How are Papa's roses doing, Margaret?" he asked, grinning.

One year, a college boy was hired to help with the hybridization. Mrs. Pullen kept an eye on him and finally decided it was her duty to warn Boerner that the youth was doing the roses wrong. In tagging the plants, he was twisting the wires so tightly that the circulation of the sap was cut off. Gene listened, but perhaps he put the remark down to professional jealousy. At any rate, he did nothing about it. When the season was farther advanced and it was obvious that none of the new assistant's crosses were taking, he called Margaret in and pointed out the error.

"But I told you, Mr. Gene. Don't you remember? I came and warned you."

"Yes, you told me. But why didn't you make me listen?"

Another time, a college girl hired to help with the hybridizing decided to make some crosses on her own, rather than following Boerner's decisions. "I had to squeal on her," Mrs. Pullen said. "Gene told me, 'You take your knife and cut 'em all off.' "

When he went hybridizing, Boerner's custom was to wear a white carpenter's apron with large pockets to carry such tools as the brushes, pill boxes, and tweezers. The female parent was prepared for the cross by doing away with its bisexuality. Its petals and stamens were removed, leaving only the female organs, the calyx, styles, and stigmas. A clean camel's-hair brush was used for each cross, then sterilized in alcohol before being used again so there would be no doubt about the identity of the parent. After pollen was brushed on the stigmas, Boerner sometimes explained to visitors, microscopic tubes descended from the pollen grains through the stigmas and the styles to the ovary, fertilizing the eggs. These became the seeds, contained in the small pod known as the hip.

Boerner estimated that three out of four such crosses produced seeds. If the cross was successful, the hip was ripe and ready to be picked in about three months. In the early days germination had taken about four times as long. The waiting period was cut by storing the plants in a cooler, fooling the seeds into supposing it was winter. After germinating in the cooler, the seedlings were placed in flats, boxes about four inches deep, filled with peat moss.

Later they were transplanted to two-inch pots, one plant per pot. At this stage, some of the plants produced tiny flowers. Normally it was impossible to tell from these whether the rose was a likely candidate. But now and then Boerner got a hunch based on such shaky evidence, as in the case of a rose he began to develop in the 1940s. Something about this tiny seedling made him believe he had a winner. Sure enough, it became Golden Masterpiece, which he considered one of his best hybrid teas.

After the seedlings were moved to larger pots, they grew to the height of a foot or more and put out flowers. These seldom looked like much, but from long experience and the habit of studying the plants daily he was able at this stage to form a judgment about which new varieties were most apt to prove useful. A casual visitor saw only the flowers, but Gene looked for other things as well — tiny differences in the leaves and stems, even the thorns.

When he saw a rose that seemed to be heading in the direction of the goal he had in mind, he might use that seedling as the female parent and cross it with the variety that he had used for its male parent, an incestuous arrangement that strengthened the qualities he sought. The process might be repeated into the fifth or sixth generation, crossing and recrossing the same stock until the result was a new rose capable of holding its own in the marketplace.

It was a frustrating as well as a fascinating sort of game. If some way could be found to make roses reproduce true from seed, the process could be simplified immensely. But there was no way of telling whether the true Mendelian response could be expected from any particular cross. Of a dozen seeds from the same pod it was unlikely any two would be alike. "This instability often drives a rose hybridist almost crazy," Boerner told a visitor, "but it also presents him with a challenge. He may always spot an unsuspected winner if he's constantly on the alert, even if it's not the exact hybrid he was trying for." His favorite examples of a rose's unpredictability were those famous unlike twins, Fashion and Vogue. These outstanding roses came from seeds found in the same rose hip, so their heredity could be presumed to be identical. But Vogue was cherry red and Fashion a coral peach, among other notable differences.

The early weeding-out process got rid of about seventy per cent of the annual crop of seedlings. Survivors which looked promising for outdoor culture were put in the fields in what were called experimental blocks. Each day Boerner walked past to take note of their progress, scribbling notes to himself or, in later years, talking into a tape recorder. After a year or two of such observation a few of the seedlings in the blocks were picked for the test gardens. Most of the others were eventually discarded, but now and then a rose was kept in the limbo of the experimental blocks for as much as ten years if Boerner felt it had sufficient promise but the market was wrong for its introduction.

The experimental blocks were some distance from the greenhouses. To get to them, Gene drove past plantings of poppies or daisies, primroses or Monardas, their multi-colored blooms interspersed with the green fields and stands of evergreens. In one field were rows of wild multifloras, used for understock. The Newark fields did not compare in size with those the company owned in California or, later, in Arizona. At any given moment, there were a mere million-and-a-half rose bushes in the New York fields, compared to perhaps ten million at the western locations. Growing the bushes at widely-separated locations made it unlikely that unfavorable weather would hamper production. Besides, it was easier to find the seasonal labor needed by dividing the crop in three parts. The western establishments had the advantage of a longer growing season, so the bushes could be planted about three months earlier than in Newark.

The work of propagation was carried on in the fields by two-man teams, a budder and his apprentice. Branches about a foot long, taken from the hybrid rose to be propagated, were carried in a wooden box. Each branch stripped of its leaves, contained perhaps a dozen eyes. The budder used a sharp knife to cut off a shield-shaped portion of the bark about an inch long, with an eye at the center. Then he made a T-shaped cut in the stem of the understock below the bush's lowest branch,

parting the bark at the intersection of the two incisions with a knife blade, prying it back so he could insert the bud into the cut. His helper bound the wound with a rubber band after the bark had been replaced so only the eye showed, and the budding was finished.

If all went well, such a bud became part of the parent plant less than three weeks later. It normally stayed dormant until the following spring, when the understock was cut back to about an inch above the bud so the root system would pour all its strength into the bud and encourage it to send out shoots which became the stems of the plant. By the following fall the bush would be large enough to be dug and stored for shipment.

The final phase of the hybridizing program took place in the nursery's two test gardens, where the most promising bushes were kept for two years or more before a final decision was made by Boerner and Perkins. The first test garden might have half a dozen examples of as many as five thousand varieties at any given time. Of these, perhaps three hundred would be found worthy of being moved to the second test garden and of being tried in a hundred testing stations in all parts of the country. These outside testers were mostly amateur but expert gardeners. If fifty or sixty per cent of them liked a rose, that was not good enough. But if eight of ten were enthusiastic, it was likely to be marketed, providing that Boerner had detected no flaw.

In his hybridizing, Gene hoped to create roses that would be able to contend with insects and plant diseases as well as cold climates.

"Just as the firmness of rose petals has been brought into the florists' roses, so can more disease and insect resistance be bred into the outdoor roses of today," he predicted. "Some varieties are untouched by insects while all around them are plants badly chewed or their leaves ruined by mites. There are certain floribundas which the Japanese beetle does not like. By patient breeding this quality can be brought into all roses. There are also varieties that are not liked by the red spider mite. The ideal rose, of course, brings its foliage to the soil level and keeps it there all summer."

During the 1940s he concentrated much of his attention in hybridizing to creating roses with more health and vigor. "The present breeding of the floribunda roses is heading toward disease resistance, hardiness, and a liberal inclusion of fragrance," he reported, although new colors were also being developed.

The All-America Rose Selections, he felt, properly emphasized the need of plants which required less-expert care. In discussing the outlook during the immediate postwar period, he predicted that the future of the rose world was both interesting and secure. "The fields to be explored are many. One of the greatest is that of hardiness. The hybridizer is again challenged, for since hardiness without beauty becomes strictly utilitarian and has little lift for the soul, it is up to the hybridizer to continue his work until he combines the two and has the rose of the North with as much beauty as the rose of the more tender climates."

Chapter XIII

Celebrities Among The Hybrids

It was in 1931, the Depression's nadir, when Jackson & Perkins launched what was to become its most distinctive method of promoting roses in general and J. & P. roses in particular. The annual rose festival started on a modest scale that year. It grew into an event that attracted hundreds of thousands of visitors a year to the small and somewhat out-of-the-way community. Before long, Newark was bragging on large billboards that it was the Rose Capital of the World. The festival grew out of an annual children's parade organized by Newark merchants. As the most promotion-minded of the local businessmen, Charlie Perkins naturally took a hand, gradually transforming the character of the annual celebration. As the festival progressed beyond its tentative beginnings, some of those at the nursery felt it was getting out of hand. Its leading opponent was Dr. Nicolas, who complained he was being driven frantic by all those strangers who peered over his shoulder while he was examining the results of his hybridizing.

The Perkins brothers and Boerner discussed the matter and decided Dr. Nick had a point: The casual visitors did not belong in the test gardens. But the opportunity to promote roses was too good to give up. It was decided to create a special display garden where tourists could amble around, looking at roses, without annoying Nicolas or otherwise getting underfoot. Seventeen acres across from the company head-quarters were set aside for a project that was completed in 1935. Dr. Nicolas no longer had to brush off all those amateurs. The visitors could see rose bushes laid out in an artistically-designed garden. Some of the strollers might be inspired to go home and create rose gardens of their own. If they used Jackson & Perkins bushes for that purpose, so much the better.

Despite the war, which made travel difficult, sixty thousand rose lovers showed up for the annual June festival in 1942. Boerner made it a point to eavesdrop on the visitors' comments, seeking clues as to whether a particular variety being tested should be discarded or added to the catalogue. Three years later, with the war nearly over and hopes for postwar expansion of the rose business rising high, it was decided that the display garden should be expanded and improved. Alfred L. Boerner, then President of the Chicago chapter of the Society of American Landscape Architects, was chosen to prepare the plans and oversee the job. The choice of Gene's kid brother to design the rose garden was not a case of rampant nepotism but a tribute to Al Boerner's reputation as a landscape architect. In Wisconsin he had shared with an old Socialist named Charles B. Whitnall the credit for creating one of the nation's finest park systems.

Alfred L. Boerner Botanical Gardens, Whitnall Park, Milwaukee, Wisconsin.

In 1926, when Alfred was twenty-eight years old and employed as Milwaukee County's landscape architect, he and Whitnall, then a vigorous seventy-one, tramped around a section of farm land ten miles southwest of the city and talked of creating a botanical garden there. By 1930 they had persuaded the county supervisors to buy a 655-acre tract, its north section set aside for the botanical garden. Four years later, when Roosevelt's New Dealers were developing nearby Greendale as one of a series of "greenbelt housing projects," the federal government gave the county another 800 acres for park and parkway purposes. Most of this land became an addition to what was by now being called Whitnall Park. Some 450 acres were set aside for the botanical gardens, including an arboretum.

Celebrities Among the Hybrids

Planting was begun, the goal being to include every plant native to the region along with a number of more exotic varieties. The botanical display included a rock garden, a perennial garden, an herb garden and — inevitably, with a Boerner in charge — a rose garden. Eventually this Wisconsin rose garden grew to contain five thousand bushes of more than three hundred fifty varieties, many of them gifts from Jackson & Perkins. Gene made his brother's projects one of the company's test gardens, which not only suited the Milwaukee taxpayers but gave J.&.P. a chance to test its roses in one of the world's most difficult winter climates. With Gene Boerner busily trying to produce roses that would thrive in his native Wisconsin and Al Boerner helping develop the park into a midwestern showplace, it was a useful arrangement for everyone concerned. Alfred Boerner later rose to head the Milwaukee County park system, and after his death in 1955 the botanical gardens he had created were named in his honor.

The rose garden at the Boerner Arboretum is one of the nation's finest, attracting about a million visitors a year, but the one which Alfred designed for his brother's company outdistanced it. With thirty-six thousand bushes on seventeen acres, it formed a magnificent show-piece for Jackson & Perkins' principal product. Most of the roses were those being sold in current catalogues. Some were the most promising of the new varieties being tested. Another section of the garden, called a "living library," reminded visitors of the rose's ancient history. Varieties which most gardeners had never seen were planted there, among

Visitors to the Jackson & Perkins Rose Festival admire the colorful beds featuring many of Gene Boerner's creations.

113

them the Rosa monstrosa, a green rose that had been hybridized two centuries earlier. Its flowers were a sickly bronze green, and even such a confirmed rose lover as Boerner conceded that it was homely. But it was a landmark in the long history of mankind's efforts to alter nature.

With half a million dollars allotted for the new rose garden, Alfred Boerner was able to create an oasis of beauty. Rose beds were massed along both sides of a four-hundred-foot mall which led to the steps of a garden house where visitors could relax and look out on a pool with a fountain playing. To the sides were individual rose gardens, each small enough so a visiting gardener could imagine it transported to his own backyard. One such garden combined climbers and hybrid teas, floribundas and pigmy roses, with the climbers draping themselves over a split-rail fence. A garden designed for children featured varieties of the Pinocchio family in a small Court of Honor with three flagpoles and a bird bath.

By rough estimate more than half a million visitors a year journeyed to Newark to walk through this garden, as many as two hundred thousand of them during the last two weeks of June when the rose festival was held. The garden served as the setting for ceremonies attended by such celebrities as Thomas E. Dewey, the governor who was twice a presidential candidate; Rose Bampton, the opera star; and Mary Margaret McBride, whose name was then at least as familiar to radio fans as the others. When a rose was named for this broadcasting star, her followers regarded it as no more than her due.

Another ceremony held at the garden involved a fictitious character who was thought of as a flesh-and-blood person by some of her millions of admirers. At the 1952 festival the Ma Perkins rose was dedicated to that motherly myth during a broadcast of her soap opera, an example of Jackson & Perkins' periodic flirtation with show biz. Ma's rose was a salmon-pink floribunda Gene had created by crossing Fashion with Red Radiance. It was duly christened while millions of listeners huddled close to their radios. Ma herself, in the person of an actress named Virginia Payne, was suitably humble though proud of the honor. The pride was justified the following year when the Ma Perkins rose won an All-America title.

The broadcast from the rose garden began with Announcer Dan Donaldson reminding Ma's listeners that Banker Pendleton had finally been persuaded to see a lawyer after Matilda Pendleton made some nasty charges against him and Mrs. Mackenzie in a divorce suit. "But something quite different is happening today. You remember that a couple of weeks back, Ma got a letter from a Mr. Perkins saying how he had named a new rose the 'Ma Perkins' rose and inviting her to Newark, New York, for Ma Perkins Day to celebrate the introduction of this new rose. Well, today is the day! And now we take you to Newark and Dallas Townsend of CBS News."

Townsend said that a few weeks before he had described an atomic bomb blast in New Mexico, the latest development in the art of war. "Today I am in Newark to bring you a quite different occasion, one much closer to the hearts of men. We are here today to do honor to a little old lady and to a flower...." After quite a bit of further ado, he turned the mike over to Charlie Perkins, who said he was "mighty proud to claim kinship with Ma Perkins" because she stood for qualities "which go to the very core of American life." Then he introduced Ma, who said "thank you," and Boerner, who said "how do you do" to all of Ma's fans.

Townsend interviewed Gene, who explained briefly what a hybridist did, how the floribunda was "the rose of the future" and how a new rose was tested in all sections of the country. Finally, Ma Perkins got a bouquet of her roses and a chance at the microphone. "I don't believe anything so nice has happened to me in my whole life," she quavered in the voice known to millions. "You know, when you get to my time of life, you find yourself lookin' back, thinking about the good things — and the sad things, too — trying to figure out what your life has meant. And I think most all of us find that it's...it's been good. There's things that ain't been so good, of course, but we learn so much. And I think maybe the most important thing we learn is to love one another...."

Ma meandered on for some little time, but eventually the philosophizing ended, the applause rose and died, and life on the CBS network returned to normal with Dan Donaldson promising that tomorrow "Ma will be on her way back to Rushville Center and the problems of the Pendleton family. And we meet the Pendletons' new lawyer — to everyone's pleasure, except Joseph's — tomorrow."

Even when the celebrities attracted by the annual rose festival were not quite as famous as Ma Perkins, there was plenty for the visitors to see there. A Rose Princess was crowned. Children got prizes for costumes made of roses. Flower arrangers competed for a bowl donated by the Sterling Silversmiths Guild of America. Eastman Kodak sent representatives to explain how to photograph roses on Camera Day. Department store models walked through the garden in the latest styles, each carrying a rose bouquet that matched her dress. Amateur gardeners competed for prizes. Owners of old cars drove around in their antique flivvers.

When Boerner could talk about roses, he was in his glory. He liked to mingle with strangers as well as friends, and the festivals brought a plentiful supply of both. Some of the more important guests were entertained on Charlie Perkins' lawn or taken through the company headquarters, portions of which looked more like the back room of a florist's shop than the center of operations of the nation's largest rose-grower. Perkins' office, for instance, was lined with shelves that held fertilizers and dusting powders as well as books. The books themselves had to do with roses and how to grow them in the face of all the natural hazards to which they were heir. As Perkins peered at his visitors through gold-rimmed spectacles, chewing on an unlit cigar, the conversation was apt to be about such practical matters as rose thrips or black spot, the shortage of rain, or the overabundance of chilly weather.

By late spring each year much of the activity around Newark was aimed at the rose festival, which depended not only on the skills of the gardeners but on the vagaries of Nature. There were years when Nature refused to cooperate by providing the sun and rain needed to bring the flowers into bloom in time for all those June visitors. But somehow the garden usually turned out to be lovely when the time came.

One year, however, the early June temperatures had been cold enough to require the use of smudge pots to discourage frost, and on the eve of the show J.&P. broadcast messages over Rochester and Syracuse radio stations asking people to postpone their visits because the roses were only in bud, not in bloom. The warning was ignored. The crowd was as large as ever, even though chilly rains soaked 4-H queens and crepe paper decorations alike.

Along with all the promotional activities, the festivals were an excuse for rosarians to get together and talk about their favorite topic. Even such distinguished hybridists as Wilhelm Kordes showed up on occasion, giving Gene a chance not only to show off the gardens and his roses but to get down to detailed speculations about plant heredity or ways of breeding greater disease resistance into the bushes. He and Kordes spent hours walking through the test gardens, talking roses, stooping to peer at those bushes where the foliage was properly healthy from top to bottom or to get a closer look at an opening bud.

The festivals were busy times at Gene's Landing, the cobblestone house on Seneca Lake where Boerner now lived. Originally named Earl's Landing for Jephthah Earl, a brewer who built it in 1835, the one-hundred-sixty-acre farm had once been a way station for steamboats that negotiated the canals and Finger Lakes with cargoes of coal and grain. Earl had lived there only a few years. During the hard times of 1837, beer sales fell off, and Jephthah found he could no longer afford to be a country squire. By the time Boerner bought the place more than a century later, the house built from stones picked up along the shore of the lake had passed through numerous hands and was in need of repair.

It had a number of obvious drawbacks when Gene first moved in. The eleven-hundred-foot frontage on Seneca Lake was an asset, particularly to a man who would almost as soon catch fish as tend roses. But the house was separated from the water by a rural road and a railroad track. The farm's soil had lost its natural fertility from years of neglect. For some years the place had been operated by tenants who had not seen fit to waste money on fertilizer. "The place had been mined, not farmed," Gene's sister, Helene, said in describing the conditions that prevailed when he moved in.

Obtaining enough water for the house's three bathrooms was another problem that proved both annoying and expensive to solve. At first Boerner had to buy water by the tank truckload and the truck sometimes had to come every other day. Several wells were drilled, one of them to the impressive depth of seven hundred feet, but the water was unsatisfactory even at this level. There were rumors of oil under the property, but Gene would have settled for an adequate supply of water. The shortage was not solved until he had a main buried beneath the road and railroad track, then pumped water up the hill to the house by means of two gasoline-powered engines.

The cobblestone house at Penn-Yan, a community named for Pennsylvanians and Yankees who first settled there, had numerous advantages to go along with its problems, however. Its location thirty miles from Newark gave him a chance to get away from the routine and find the relaxation he needed. Equally important, Gene's Landing fulfilled an ambition kept green ever since those boyhood days in Wisconsin when his grandmother's farm represented one principal center of his world. He had the country boy's need for uncluttered space around him.

The farm was more suitable to a nature lover than a farmer when he bought it, but Boerner was too good a horticulturist to be content for long with infertile soil. He bought fertilizer by the truckload and ordered it spread over his fields. For the first few years, he planted nothing but soybeans, a legume which could add nitrogen to the depleted soil. Then he went in for strip farming, added six acres of grapes, dug a pond.

Gene's Landing on Seneca Lake near Penn Yan, N.Y. in the autumn when some of his prize chrysanthemums were still in bloom.

Celebrities Among the Hybrids

The love affair with Nature that the Boerner children had begun in the Wisconsin countryside was a factor in his decision to move to Gene's Landing. There were black raspberries, blackberries, wild apple trees, and crabapples growing on the farm, not to mention an old walnut tree in the front yard that had grown so mighty that travelers sometimes stopped their cars to gaze at it in amazement. As he had done when he was a boy, Boerner kept track of the resident birds and was delighted when he saw a deer cross his lawn.

The ground floor of the cobblestone house included a living room and dining room with big windows on the lake side and a kitchen with a fireplace. Some years after he bought the place, he added a sleeping wing which he called his dormitory, designed mostly for young visitors, especially nieces and nephews. His own bedroom was upstairs. From its windows he could look down a long, grassy slope to the lake. To the south were the vineyards. The grapes were sold to a nearby winery, which always arranged for a case or two of champagne to be delivered to him.

Boerner added barns for the Herefords he acquired, thus fulfilling another boyhood ambition, the vow to have cattle when he grew up but not cows that needed to be milked. As a gentleman farmer who planned to build up one of the region's finest herds, he admired the blooded stock he owned, but his favorite livestock turned out to be somewhat smaller,

Gene spends a few minutes with his affectionate dachshunds.

dachshunds. Faust was the first, acquired on a trip to Germany. Bachelorhood suited Boerner, but he soon decided Faust needed a mate. So Rita arrived, shipped by a German breeder to Newark. The dogs' first litter arrived on a Fourth of July, so inevitably one of the pups had to bear up under the name of Independence. Like many childless persons, Boerner began to look on his pets as something more than dumb beasts. Even his friends admitted that each dachshund had a distinctive personality. Faust got lonely when his master was gone, or so Gene thought, at any rate. Until Rita arrived, Faust usually rode along with Boerner to his office and accompanied him wherever he went during the day. Boerner's friends soon learned more about dachshunds than some of them cared to know.

A member of the second litter, a female named Sherry, turned out to be the problem child of the lively group. Sherry was in the habit of going hunting by herself and tackling game far out of a dachshund's proper weight class. She was always coming home full of bites and claw marks from an encounter with a woodchuck, and Gene would rush her to the vet, Dr. D.W. Pulver, at nearby Phelps, to be patched up. Sherry never learned she was too small to whip a woodchuck, however, and a few weeks later Boerner's car would arrive in a cloud of dust at the veterinarian's office, and in he would come bearing his prodigal pup once more.

Dr. Pulver also kept a professional eye on the Boerner herd, which began with a number of steers and progressed to a collection of purebred Herefords, some of which had been imported at considerable expense from Cody, Wyoming.

There were times when Gene wanted to get off by himself, one step removed from even the haven of the big cobblestone house, so he bought a camping trailer and parked it on the beach of his lakefront property, staying there for a day or two when life began to get on his nerves. It wasn't as secluded as the hawthorn grove at Cedarburg where he'd spent boyhood summers with his brothers and sister, but it served.

The big house was always kept well stocked with food, ready to entertain the guests that Boerner liked to have around him. But he was no housekeeper, and sometimes he lost track of domestic details. One summer, for example, a barrel of clams that had been put in the cooler for some future feast was forgotten until they had spoiled and had to be thrown out.

Gene liked to supply his friends and colleagues with fresh fruit and produce from the farm or fish from the lake. Mrs. Margaret Pullen recalls one occasion when he asked her to come out to the house and help

Gene proudly displays a dolphin caught off Key Largo, Flordia.

him deal with a particularly large catch. "He had me down there in the cooler sorting out fish," she said. "This fish for Louis, that fish for so-and-so. Even I had to take one — and I don't like fish." In season, the back of his car was likely to be loaded with country produce when he arrived at the company headquarters. "He was always giving us grapes, eggs, various things," Mrs. Pullen said. "You never knew what you were going to get next."

Since boyhood, Boerner had collected aphorisms the way some men collect stamps, and one of his favorites was a couplet that went:

"To make a living, foul or fair,
"One cannot farm from a swivel chair."

But at Gene's Landing, he realized, that was a fairly close description of what he was doing. He was too busy to heed his own poetic advice and had to depend on hired help, some of whom worked out better than others. He always hoped to put the farm on a paying basis, but it remained a hobby and an expensive one. In 1948, for example, he sold nearly $5,000 worth of hay, grain, and soybeans, but the farm's expenses were over $8,000. In 1954, a year when he made extensive purchases of cattle, his deficit from farming ran to nearly $12,000. By then, he could afford such luxuries, his salary having climbed to about $27,000 a year, augmented by company profits and a profitable stock portfolio. During the 1940s, with Jackson & Perkins' business expanding as Americans headed by the millions for suburbia and lots large enough to tempt them to plant rose bushes, Boerner's income tripled.

During the early forties he hired Jim Emerson, a neighbor, to take care of the farm chores. Emerson's wife, Pauline, and her sister, Sara Oaks, took care of the housecleaning. This was apparently considered more skilled labor than the farm chores, for at a time when Emerson was working outdoors for fifty cents an hour, his wife and sister-in-law were being paid seventy-five cents an hour for their part-time housework.

When Boerner was away from home on one of his numerous trips, Pauline Emerson and Mae Cooper, Gene's secretary, kept up a steady stream of chatty letters about the details of running Gene's Landing. Miss Cooper — later, Mrs. Mae Lunay — had become Boerner's secretary after he took over Dr. Nicolas' responsibilities and remained with him in that capacity for the rest of his career. His bluff outspokenness was resented by some, but she admired him as "a man who was always thinking, always planning" and managed to get along with him just fine. She became his indispensable alter ego, sometimes knowing what he wanted to do before he knew himself. Her duties were various, ranging from routine secretarial work to making sure the farm was operating smoothly while its owner was sniffing roses in Europe.

The Emersons continued to help out until 1950. Then, with Boerner getting deeper into the cattle business, he decided he needed a full-time foreman. A series of men were hired. For one reason or another they came and went. The last of the series was Robert Generaux, who took over responsibility for the Herefords and continued a sometimes stormy relationship with his boss until the cattle were auctioned off in the mid-1960s.

As a part-time country squire, Boerner made friends with his neighbors and was called on for advice about their landscaping problems. When the Henry Christensens built a new house in 1951 to replace one that had burned down, he offered to take charge of the planting. As might have been expected, the emphasis was on floribundas, mostly those which he had developed himself. To the right of the Christensen front door, he planted Siren, a dark red Kordes rose which J. & P. was planning to market in 1953. With it he planted Glacier, a new white

Ma Perkins, Floribunda (1952)

floribunda Gene had developed by crossing Summer Snow with an unnamed hybrid tea. To the left he planted Fashion and another of his All-America winners, Ma Perkins. On the south side of the house he combined a number of varieties, including Siren, Summer Snow, and Pinocchio. Edna Christensen said she was especially fond of yellow, so Gene gave her a bed of hybrid teas named Golden Masterpiece which she could see whenever she looked out of her kitchen window. This flower bed also included New Yorker and Rome Glory, with a small floribunda named Pigmy Red for edging. Flanking the back door were an improved version of Blaze and another climber, Coral Dawn, which Boerner patented in 1952.

When Don Cunnion, a writer for *Country Gentleman,* showed up in Newark to get material for an article about roses, Boerner escorted him to the Christensen home to illustrate how floribundas could be used in landscaping. "They provide a maximum display of color for beauty at a minimum of cost and care," Gene told him. "Floribundas fill practically every requirement of the average home rose-grower, the person who loves roses but who hasn't much time to spend caring for them."

S.D. McGredy, managing director of Samuel McGredy & Sons Royal Nurseries at Portadown, Northern Ireland, was among the European hybridists who visited him at Gene's Landing. By now many of the rose growers he met on his European trips were his close friends. They looked forward to talking with this ebullient American who combined a businessman's sense of the practicalities of making money with a genuine love of flowers. McGredy was amused by Boerner's habit of popping a rose under his hat and walking around for a while before removing the flower and sniffing it to test its fragrance. What was needed to bring out the flower's aroma, Gene explained, was "a very close atmosphere," and where better to find such an atmospheric condition than under his own fedora? McGredy also noted that Boerner often put roses in his briefcase, carrying them around for days to see how long they would retain their beauty out of water.

Roses were not the only things he put under his hat. Walking around his acreage on a hot day, Gene sometimes stuffed a handful of wet grass there to keep his head cool, then forgot it was there. When he arrived at the office and took off his hat, the grass would fall out. Dried wisps of hay might stay in his hair for hours, to the secret amusement of visitors and the office help.

One reason for buying Gene's Landing was that Boerner wanted a place where he could entertain on a scale that recaptured the *gemuetlich* atmosphere of those boyhood dinners he remembered in Wisconsin. As was natural for a man who had grown up in the calorie-laden atmosphere of pre-World War I Cedarburg, food was an important pleasure. He enjoyed it, which made him not only a welcome guest when he traveled but an excellent host. No one went hungry for long in the cobblestone house overlooking the lake, just as no one's appetite had been neglected in the days when the Boerner women vied in friendly competition to supply the tastiest desserts for those Sundays at Grandma Oma's. At Gene's Landing he had not one but three large freezers in the basement, and he never felt quite comfortable unless all three were full of provisions. Capons were a particular favorite. He might keep as many as one hundred of the frozen birds on hand at a time, waiting their turn in the oven.

Some visitors, particularly the feminine ones, felt that something was missing in this handsome country house. What he needed, they dared hint now and then, was a wife. He either pretended not to understand or passed off the suggestion with a joke. As a young man, there had been numerous girls; and when he grew older, he had a succession of women friends, some of whom no doubt considered this prosperous fellow a likely catch. But he enjoyed his bachelor freedom too much, including the ability to pack his bag and leave at a moment's notice. There were various theories among his friends and relatives about his reasons for leaving marriage out of his plans — "he was too busy making money," one said, for example. But his brother, Carl, had another explanation: "He was having too good a time."

His closest friend during his years at Gene's Landing was a Cornell economist, Prof. Frank A. Pearson, whose views on the revaluation of the dollar had been much in the news during the 1930s Depression. Boerner read an article about Pearson's economic theories in 1935, was intrigued by them, and got on the telephone to invite the professor and his wife to Sunday dinner. The Pearsons arrived just as Gene had finished cooking a capon. It turned out to be a marvelous meal, all of it prepared by their host, and the wine list was equally impressive. Pearson was as outspoken as Boerner, and the two got on so well that this Sunday dinner turned into a series of such meals that went on for more than thirty years.

Boerner remained close to his brothers and sister, who visited him often. In addition to those annual Christmas trips to Wisconsin, Gene often went on fishing expeditions, particularly with Alfred or Robert Boerner, heading north into Wisconsin or Canada. On one such trip, Gene caught a large muskie. He had it mounted and hung in the

New Yorker, Hybrid Tea (1947)

dormitory wing. His sister considered it "a hideous thing with a red mouth," but she did not look at it from a fisherman's viewpoint. Gene regarded it as almost as beautiful as a rose.

The Finger Lake country reminded Boerner of Wisconsin, with its rolling hills and numerous small bodies of water. He liked to sit at his bedroom window or walk down to the lake shore to watch the seasonal flights of geese and ducks or look in admiration at a storm sweeping toward him over the lake. The old house gave him a feeling of being part of the history of this lovely region. He found an 1844 drawing of the place — white board fences, young trees growing, cows grazing in the front yard, the house looking much the same as now — and he used it as an illustration for one of a series of Christmas cards which he sent to hundreds of friends and acquaintances throughout the world.

Christmas had always meant a lot to him, and he went to considerable trouble to make his annual holiday messages stand out from the commercialized sentiment that flooded the mails each December. He took pains to choose an appropriate picture to illustrate the card — one, for example, showed four dachshunds romping in the snow beneath the big walnut tree in front of his house — and gave equal attention to picking a message to accompany the drawing or photograph. These ranged from the whimsical — "May your cookie jar always be full" — to the philosophical. For example, "A strong friend is a strong defense; he that hath found one hath found a treasure," or the one chosen to accompany the 1844 version of the cobblestone house: "The ornament of a house is the friends who grace it."

His Christmas card list eventually grew to four-hundred-fifty names. All during the year, Boerner was on the lookout for a suitable verse or axiom, jotting them down or setting aside a clipping. When autumn came, the season which brings an annual crisis of the spirit for gardeners when the death or annual hibernation of growing things has its effect, he would call up Horace Howard, editor of the *Newark Courier*. Bump Howard learned to expect the annual summons. "When you have a few moments, editor, come on up and we'll mull this problem over."

Then Bump and Gene would sit over a cup of coffee, choosing among Boerner's harvest of clippings and notations, deciding which was worthy to carry the load of his Christmas greeting. It was an annual ritual that both men enjoyed. "In the rose business, everybody else seemed commercial," Howard said, looking back on those days. "But you didn't get that feeling with Gene. That guy was dedicated to the quintessence of beauty. Genial Gene — he had a passion for the best of anything including friendship."

Another custom, carried over from his childhood, was the baking of Christmas cookies. The thought of the aromas that had risen in December kitchens in Cedarburg returned to him; and now that he was no longer able to go to Grandma Oma's to nibble on the wonderful variety of cookies available there, he baked them himself. He took pride in this skill. Before long, his international reputation as a creator of new roses was bolstered by an impressive reputation as a cookie-baker. As early as 1941, he shared some of his recipes with readers of *House Beautiful*. Unfortunately, he forgot to mention that in baking a batch of "Sand Tortes" three eggs were needed, an omission that caused consternation in kitchens throughout the land.

About ten years later, he tried again. With advice from his sister — by then, the widow of the Rev. E. Benjamin Schlueter — he put together a booklet of favorite recipes, complete with the necessary number of eggs this time. He accompanied them with philosophical observations on cookie-baking and its attendant skill, cookie-eating.

"I have always had a preference for the old style procedure of baking. This required frequent opening of the oven's door and kept the house saturated with fine, spicy fragrances. The new methods worked out by the present generation, graduates of home economics schools, give temperatures and times — and take all the fun out of it. I never do have a chance at scorched pans of cookies any more.

"...Have you ever tried the real brown peppernuts (Pfeffernusse)? These are made with lots of ginger, cloves, all-spice, black pepper, and rolled into long, thin fingers and cut off in half-inch lengths and baked hard. Try some, letting them disintegrate on your tongue. Have a good book in your hand and then try to stop eating them.

"...A very sensible thing to do is to get right down to baking some of these cookies. Be sure to supply yourself with ample tins and jars before you start, for you'll never be able to save them for Christmas unless you do. If there are any youngsters in the house, I'd suggest having one jar where it might be reached with the aid of a chair; it's always fun to do it."

He didn't mention it in the booklet, but there had been just such a jar in his grandmother's pantry. It might be a closed tin box one year, a stone crock the next, but it was always hidden high in a cupboard so that when Gene was small, he'd been forced to put a stool on top of a chair to gain the required altitude for reaching in and swiping some of the secret horde. In those days he had supposed he was getting away with something, making the cookies from the hidden store taste best of all. But now he knew better. He was sure that Oma had known all along how her cookies were disappearing and had put them there for that very purpose with love.

Chapter XIV

Pinocchio Gets Married

Creating and distributing new roses was a business, a matter of dollars and cents, a subject for clever promotion schemes and the competitive game of economics. But roses were something more than a product to Boerner. Improving them was also an art, his hope for a measure of immortality. He liked to think of his floral children going down through the years long after he had been forgotten, passing on their inheritance to roses yet unborn, roses not yet even imagined.

There in the big house at Penn-Yan he spent much of his spare time browsing through books of rose lore and an even more specialized form of literature, the rose cookbooks. For example, he collected recipes from *The Cook and Housewife's Manual* by Mrs. Christian Isabel Johnstone, published in Scotland in 1837, and *Adam's Luxury and Eve's Cookery, or The Kitchen Garden Displayed,* published in London on Paternoster Row in 1744. "Take one pound of rose buds," the latter volume advised, "and bruise them with a wooden pestle in a marble mortar, adding by degrees of white loaf-sugar powdered and sifted, three pounds, continue beating them till no particles of the rose can be seen and till the mass is all alike." The result was called Conserve of Red Roses.

American authors had not ignored the usefulness of the rose in cookery. Gene discovered *Miss Beecher's Domestic Recipe Book*, published in New York in 1851, with its advice to gather rose leaves and preserve them "by crowding them in a jar with brandy" to be used in cooking. Then there was *Housekeeping in Old Virginia*, published in Richmond in 1878, containing contributions from two-hundred-fifty southern ladies. It told how to prepare "eye water for weak eyes" by combining one teaspoon of laudanum, two teaspoonfuls of Madeira and twelve teaspoonfuls of rose water. Roses were also used in what was described as a remedy for falling hair, providing, the book noted cautiously, that baldness did not run in the family. The hair preservative included rose water, glycerine, and tincture of cantharides.

As a man able to look a calorie in the eye without flinching, Boerner admired a recipe for rose ice cream he discovered in *The Cook's Dic-*

tionary and Housekeeper's Directory, published in London in 1833. A quart of rich cream was placed in a pan and brought to a boil before a handful of fresh rose leaves was added and left to infuse for two hours. "Then, if the cream be cold," the recipe continued, "strain and pour it on the yolks of nine eggs, beat them up well, add three-quarters of a pound of powder sugar; set it on a slow fire, and stir it constantly till it thickens, taking care that it does not boil. Run it through a bolting, and when cold, color it with a little carmine dissolved in clarified sugar; put it into a sabotiere and freeze as usual."

From another book in his collection, an 1828 volume called *The Female Economist or a Plain System of Cookery for the Use of Families*, Boerner delighted in noting such home remedies as one for chapped hands. "Take a quarter of a pound of hogs' lard, without salt," it began and went on to advise that the lard be washed in plain water, then rose water before mixing it with two new-laid eggs, a large spoonful of honey, and enough oatmeal to make a paste.

There had been a time when the wealthy had purchased rose leaves by the bushel. They were strewn on floors as well as used in cookery and medicine. Many households once had a rose still, a utensil for converting rose petals into rose water. The Romans, Boerner liked to point out, had developed a wine made from roses, and in Elizabethan days the English not only drank an oily and potent concoction known as Rosa Solis, but made up a poem about it:

"We abandon all ale
"And beer that is stale,
"Rosa Solis and damnable hum...."

The Romans made rose wine by removing the lower white portion of the rose petals, sewing the rest of the blossoms into a linen bag, and immersing it in wine for seven days. Then a second sack of rose petals was added and allowed to soak for a week. Once again, the petals were removed, and a third bag of fresh petals was added, remaining in the wine for another seven days. The petals were removed, the wine was strained through a colander and, before serving, honey was added. The rose wine was more than a drink. The Romans considered it an excellent laxative.

In notes he made for use in future speeches or articles Boerner speculated that the rose was included in Babylon's celebrated hanging gardens. He was struck by the mention in Herodotus of sixty-petaled roses in King Midas' gardens in Macedonia, four hundred years before the Christian era. Then there was Seneca's account of Smyndiride, the richest of the Sybarites, who could not sleep if one petal of his bed of roses was curled. Nero squandered the equivalent of $150,000 on roses at a single feast. Marc Antony, after the battle of Actium, stabbed himself with his sword and, as he was dying, asked his girl friend, Cleopatra, to cover his tomb with roses. In the Middle Ages the rose was so much in demand that vassals often paid their lords their annual fee in the form of a basket of roses. In 1556 a bottle of rose water was considered a gift fit for Queen Mary.

Some texts in Boerner's extensive library indicated that the rose was a mere three hundred thousand years old, so he was delighted to note an archeological discovery in Oregon which pushed the horizon back considerably farther. The geologists dug up a fossil of a wild rose which had bloomed along the Crooked River about thirty-five million years ago. It was the familiar five-petaled variety, much like those still found in American hedgerows.

It was Boerner's belief that sports of such simple roses began the race of double roses well before the dawn of history. "There were always doubles as long as there were rose records," he wrote, pointing out that as early as 484 B.C. a rose with one hundred petals was described by Herodotus. The roses of the Romans generally had only twelve petals. Boerner said that "it is doubtful that any variety of rose known to the affluent patricians of Augustine Rome would be considered worthy of exhibit by florists of today."

In the early phase of its love affair with the rose Rome imported the flowers from Alexandria and Memphis during the winter. Egyptian gardeners had large fields of roses in the rich delta lands of the Nile, potting the plants and shipping them in bud to the Romans. Later, greenhouses were devised, with the first hothouse roses available in Rome about 30 A.D. This first greenhouse was not originally designed for roses but for cucumbers. Emperor Tiberius had been advised by his doctor to eat a cucumber every day to keep his melancholy away. Even in Italy cucumbers were hard to grow in winter, but some anonymous precursor of Boerner solved the problem. He invented a glassed-in pit where fresh vegetables could be grown regardless of the weather. With the emperor supplied with medicinal cucumbers, the invention was soon put to other uses, including the forcing of roses to bloom in the winter. Seneca, for one, did not approve. "Do not those men live contrary to the will of Nature who long for a rose in winter and heat up water and adjust its warmth to force out a lily of spring among the snows?" he demanded.

Sure enough, Rome fell to the barbarians. The greenhouse was one of numerous amenities that disappeared. By the thirteenth century, however, it was in use again; a Dominican named Albertus Magnus was accused of black magic because he could make flowers grow in winter. By the seventeenth century a modification of the greenhouse was popular in France and England. Buildings called orangeries made it possible to grow tropical fruits in some unlikely locales, giving the rich and powerful one more way to show off their wealth.

After Rome's decline, the leaders in rose culture were the Moors in Spain. It was said that they even managed to create a rose as blue as the sky. If so, Moorish rosarians accomplished something that modern hybridists have not been able to match although many of them, including Gene, kept seeking the elusive blue rose.

The roses of western Europe at the time of Chaucer came from Arabic gardens of the Near East. The Damask, from which rose water was distilled, came from Syria. One of its descendants was the Province rose that reached England in 1596. From India and Persia came other roses aboard Venetian and Florentine trading caravans, adding new strains to the cultivated varieties.

One of the fashions brought back from the Crusades was an admiration for the rose. Great circular windows installed in cathedrals counterfeited in multi-colored glass the pattern of the rose, which was a symbol of spiritual as well as sentimental loyalty. Before Henry VIII broke his ties with Rome, the pope sent him the Golden Rose. The roses of Lancaster and York were symbols of the rival factions which fought for his kingdom.

In more recent years, Boerner noted, Americans have been collecting old roses much as old hobbyists collect antique furniture. They searched out abandoned gardens in the Maryland and Virginia tidewater regions where roses planted in Colonial times still grew.

During his selling trips through New England in the 1920s, Boerner had made it a point to seek out historic old rose bushes. The earliest domesticated rose to be brought to America had been planted by the Spaniards in Florida, but the English settlers had also brought the flower along to provide a touch of home in this rough, new land they were attempting to conquer. Gene made a pilgrimage to the Kittery River in Massachusetts to look at a red rose bush that had been planted by some anonymous migrant from the Old World when New England was new. From such plants as this, pioneers heading west had taken cuttings. The bush near the Kittery and others like it were the ancestors of dooryard blooms across a continent.

Hothouse roses had been grown as early as 1750 in America; but, as Boerner noted in one of numerous accounts he wrote of the flower's history, "in the early 1800s, things jumped. Rosa Chenesis was rushed into pollination. The Damask perpetual and the Bourbon perpetuals were born. Then came the first hybrid perpetuals, the very fragrant Rose du Roi. Next we come to the real hybrid perpetuals — Damask perpetuals by Bourbon perpetuals by Rosa Chenensis, starting in 1837."

The Noisettes began in 1817, although Boerner felt that they had been misnamed and should have been called Champneys. The first Noisette was hybridized by John Champney of Charleston, he pointed out, but another South Carolina gardener, Philippe Noisette, got the credit although he merely "took up where Champney left off."

The tea rose was introduced to the United States about the same time as the Noisettes. The Wichuraiana was discovered in Japan by a botanist named Wichura and introduced to Europe in 1873, but an advance made by a Frenchman eight years earlier was more significant. "M. Guillot of Lyons gave us La France, a seedling of a hybrid perpetual," Boerner wrote, "and from there came the flood of hybrid teas, which has dominated the rose world up to now."

In 1890 a list of hybrid teas grown in England included only six roses, Boerner went on, but by 1900 the total had risen to sixty-five. About that time Pernet of France crossed the Austrian yellow, Rosa Foetida, with a red hybrid perpetual, Antoine Ducher, to produce the first of the Pernetianas. Nine years later, another Frenchman, Levavasseur, produced the Orleans rose and the so-called baby ramblers. By then, Jackson & Perkins had entered the picture, if only in a small way. Its cross of a Wichuraiana with a hybrid perpetual had produced the Dorothy Perkins, leader of a race of hardy climbers whose popularity rapidly spread from Newark to all parts of the rose-growing world. The addition of Pernetiana strains to the hybrid teas produced, in Boerner's estimation, "puny plants with exquisite shapes and color until America stepped in with standards which forced a change in the picture."

One result of the demand for hardier roses was the race of floribundas, the development of which was due in considerable measure to Gene Boerner. He took comfort from the feeling that he was part of a swelling tide of advancement in the rose's development. But he felt it was important that rosarians understand that the flower owed much to the past as well as to efforts such as his. "There is a place for half-forgotten roses in our gardens, just as there is for the newest varieties," he wrote. "One can greatly admire a moss rose, recalling its association with the exquisite Eugenie and the days of the French Second Empire. But one will also pause in admiration before a newly-introduced hybrid tea.... The vogue of the rose has outlived empires. It will endure for countless centuries to come."

By now Pinocchio, the Kordes rose which Boerner had rescued from Europe just before World War II, had become a principal forerunner of the floribundas which were taking over a large share of the market. After creating white and lavender variations which retained the pink rose's hardiness, Boerner began seeking a red version of Pinocchio. He crossed it with Crimson Glory. To his delight, he came up with a coral peach beauty he named Fashion, which became one of the most popular roses in history. He and Kordes speculated about where the unusual color had come from, but Boerner was never convinced that they'd found the answer. It was plain from the first, however, that the mysteries of genetics had produced a winner. Fashion proved not only beautiful but unusually hardy. During its early years, the Texas fields where it was being grown were hit by two successive cold spells that froze many of the other roses there. But Fashion took the unusual weather in stride. From then on, Boerner used it freely in his crosses, seeking to infuse its hardiness into other varieties.

After it was introduced in 1949, Fashion became the first rose ever to win nine international prizes. Nearly twenty years later it was described in an authoritative rose publication as the most widely-grown floribunda in the United States. Boerner considered Fashion an example of why rose hybridizing remained an art as well as a science, noting that "the lovely pink floribunda Pinocchio and the favorite red hybrid tea Crimson Glory gave us not a red or a pink but the graceful new coral and gold blooms of Fashion." Fashion bypassed the color and form of its parents and "reached back to the specie forbears of Pinocchio to give this intriguing color variation," he said.

Of the million or more crosses Boerner made during his career, that 1943 marriage between Pinocchio and Crimson Glory was the luckiest. From just one of the rose hips that resulted, four seeds were obtained. He planted them and up came four tiny rose plants. Two were nothing special. But the remaining pair of siblings, born of the same seed pod, turned out to be AARS winners.

Even as seedlings, they showed promise. One produced small blooms of coral-peach, the other of cherry-coral. The shades were so new and striking that Gene could hardly wait to bud the twins onto greenhouse stock for a quick check on what the full-sized blossoms would look like. The two new roses, still unnamed, survived every test. As the 1949 season approached, Charlie Perkins decided to go for broke in introducing the coral-peach half of the pair and bud it on no less than three hundred fifty thousand bushes. "If it had failed to catch on," Perkins said later, "we would've had three hundred thousand bushes to burn."

So promoting this new rose was essential; customers do not order three hundred fifty thousand of a new variety without being nudged. While Boerner and the Perkins brothers were still pondering the best way to market the rose, a stylist from Neiman-Marcus happened by to look at the Newark gardens. He was shown the coral-colored offspring of the Pinocchio-Crimson Glory cross and decided that the shade was just the thing to feature at a style show at the Dallas department store. Boerner said this suited him fine; Neiman-Marcus had a talent for getting publicity, which was what was needed for the new rose. He named it Fashion to go with the fashion show introduction. As for its sister, being saved for the 1951 season, he would call that Vogue.

Neiman-Marcus upheld its end of the bargain. It not only displayed nearly twenty-five hundred potted bushes of the new coral-peach rose throughout its store, but it paraded long-stemmed Texas beauties in dresses that matched the blooms. Women's clothing, quilts, draperies, and even handkerchiefs of the same shade were put on sale. The fashion show for Fashion attracted attention in the press, the trend set in Dallas spread, and before long the bachelor hybridist in Newark was amused to realize that he and his camel's-hair brush had influenced the buying habits of thousands of style-conscious American women.

Gardeners took to Fashion with unprecedented enthusiasm. Other growers made arrangements to produce it, paying J. & P. the required royalty. Before long the 1950 AARS winner was selling at the rate of half a million bushes a year, outdistancing even the yellow beauty, Peace, which had been the benchmark by which other roses' success was measured since its introduction to the American market in 1945 by the Conard-Pyle Co. Charlie Perkins got special satisfaction from the news that Fashion had at last forced Peace out of first place. When Vogue, Fashion's unlike twin, made its debut in 1951 and went on to capture an All-America title the following year, both Boerner and his boss were content.

As the first truly fragrant floribunda, Fashion was especially welcome to Boerner. "I want all my roses fragrant," he said. "The first thing people do with a rose is smell it." That was usually the case with him. If the scent was elusive, he might pop the blossom into his mouth to warm it so that the fragrant oil would be more volatile and he could analyze the scent more carefully. Such habits sometimes startled strangers, such as a woman he was showing through the gardens one day. He had been wearing a rosebud in his lapel, as usual, and he gallantly offered it to her. She admired it and handed it back. He thrust it into his mouth. She looked so startled that he hastily took it out again and explained. "Don't worry, I'm not going to eat it. I'm just warming it so I can smell it better."

Besides being the first fragrant floribunda, Fashion was the first of its coral-peach shade and the first to bear blooms of hybrid tea form in clusters. Each bloom had twenty-four petals, three or four times as many as most of the early floribundas. As one of Pinocchio's most distinguished daughters, Fashion passed on its inheritance to a considerable number of other Boerner roses, of which Spartan may have been the most notable. Fashion was also widely used by other hybridists, who quickly recognized its suitability for parenthood. In France, Georges Delbard crossed it with the Orleans rose to produce an orange-scarlet variety he called Diablotin. In England, Siden and Cobley crossed Fashion with Masquerade to produce Woburn Abbey. In Northern Ireland, McGredy used Fashion and one of its descendants, Ma Perkins, to produce Chanelle. Through its parent, Crimson Glory, the fragrance of Fashion could be traced back to the Damask rose, from which attar of roses is distilled, a rose with an Oriental fragrance so strong that it is said to kill unwary insects.

Although Fashion quickly became the most profitable item in the Jackson & Perkins catalogue, its career in Europe was less happy from an economic standpoint. As early as the spring of 1950 Boerner got word from the Northern Ireland nurseryman, Alex Dickson, Jr., that Dutch growers were offering budding eyes of the new rose at a fourth of the price Dickson had planned to sell them for in the British Isles under his marketing agreement with J. & P.

"In view of the competition from Holland, our sales will be virtually nil," Dickson wrote Boerner. "I simply do not understand how this can be done, and I have no doubt there must have been hidden reserves of Fashion in Holland last year. Judging from the very limited demand from the trade during the last season, I feel sure some of the English growers were getting deliveries from abroad."

"The wolves quite evidently took hold of Fashion," Boerner replied. "There is nothing much we can do now, since the different cheaper hybridizers got hold of this variety.... I hope your government will soon give you the protection of the plant patent (law), which seems to be the only alternative." Boerner suggested that he and Dickson meet with the Dutch grower at the Chelsea flower show and "maybe we can work out a solution," but Dickson reported later in the month that another Dutch grower's catalogue had arrived, listing Fashion at an even lower price, which "will completely knock the bottom out of our market."

The experience with Fashion on the international market provided an expensive lesson for Boerner and his company. While Jackson & Perkins continued to have occasional difficulties with what Gene considered piracy of their patented roses, by the time Vogue was introduced in 1951 the company had tightened the restrictions on its sale so the new variety would not be available at cut prices until it was no longer a novelty.

One problem with the European marketing of Fashion had been an inability to patent the rose in Holland because of a technicality. The experience left Gene with the feeling that his company had been robbed. "The Hollanders are a bunch of vultures," he told Dickson, "and their close neighbor, Belgium, is in the same class."

With Vogue and Fashion, Boerner now had his first two All-America floribundas to go with his two AARS winners among the hybrid teas, Katherine T. Marshall and Diamond Jubilee. Before the 1950s had ended, five more of his floribundas would win the coveted title. Capturing such important awards was one way to ensure that a new rose would fare well in the marketplace. Boerner and the Perkins brothers were also convinced that the name they chose for the rose had considerable bearing on its sale, sometimes making the difference between success and failure. The task of choosing a name was approached with great seriousness. The company had a standing offer of $100 to anyone, employee or stranger, who could come up with an acceptable designation for a new rose and hundreds of suggestions arrived annually. But it was generally Gene or another J. & P. official who suggested the name that was finally chosen. Except where the uses of publicity required a rose to be named for an individual, Boerner preferred descriptive names — Spartan for a hardy, masculine-looking floribunda, for example, or Chatter for a perky little red rose.

Gene's favorite example of how a rose's success depended on its name was Blaze, a climber introduced by J. & P. in 1932. Largely as a promotion stunt, the company ran a contest to choose a name for this sport patented by Joseph W. Kallay, a nurseryman in Painesville, Ohio. Twenty-five thousand entries were submitted and Blaze was picked, a choice that Charlie Perkins believed was responsible for the rose's phenomonal success. "There have been better red climbers since," he said a quarter century later, "but that rose still outsells them all and, as far as I can figure, all because of that name."

By trial and error Boerner learned some rules about naming roses; never name one for a politician, for example. The Governor Alfred E. Smith was introduced by J. & P. in 1933, its name chosen for reasons Gene could never understand. Al Smith had once been a popular figure whose name might have appealed to rosarians, but by 1933 he was a disgruntled elder statesman, nursing the wounds of a decisive defeat for the presidency five years before. The Governor Alfred E. Smith fell flat on its foliage and was soon dropped from the catalogue.

The President Herbert Hoover was introduced by another grower in 1930 and did well for a while. But as the Depression deepened, not even Republicans cared to be reminded of their harassed leader in the White House. As for Democratic rosarians, by the election year of 1932 they were attacking Hoover's floral namesake with hoes. Eventually, by-gones became political bygones, and the President Herbert Hoover staged a comeback. But long before that happened, Boerner had decided that hitching a rose to a politician's coat-tails was best avoided.

Naming a variety for an institution that could be helpful in pro-moting it was another matter. The practice went back at least to 1913, when the *London Daily Mail* offered one thousand pounds for the best new fragrant rose, with the understanding that the winning bush would be named for the newspaper. The rose chosen was submitted by Joseph Pernet-Ducher. The eminent Frenchman was anxious to have the thousand-pound prize, but he balked at calling his rose for a London newspaper. He had already promised to name it for Mme. Edouard Herriot, wife of a Lyons schoolteacher who later became premier. Mme. Herriot the rose must remain, he declared. After considerable cross-channel bickering, a compromise was finally reached. On the Con-tinent, the rose would continue to honor the future premier's wife but in the British Isles it would be called the Daily Mail. Boerner named none of his roses for newspapers, but he did name one for a savings and loan company. The Chicago financial institution wanted to give away a free rose bush to any citizen thrifty enough to deposit $50, and Gene supplied a hybrid tea which he called First Federal.

Such requests to name a rose in the interests of publicizing an institution or business were not uncommon, and Boerner was always ready to listen, although by no means always ready to say yes. An oil company that asked for a rose named in its honor was turned down, for example. Boerner felt that oil and roses do not mix.

Milk was another matter. When the Borden Company was preparing for its centennial and asked to have a rose named for its founder, a rose-pink hybrid tea created by Kordes was chosen by Boerner and named the Gail Borden after the dairy firm agreed to spend a generous sum promoting the rose.

To have the best chance of success, Boerner believed, a rose should have a name that was easy to remember and pronounce and, if possible, one that had pleasant connotations. When he found a rose in the McGredy test fields in Ireland that he was determined to try out, he knew at once it would have to be given a new name. The McGredy clan, little impressed by the rose, had called it The Mouse, a name Gene was sure would be hard to sell to American gardeners.

The rose was gray. When Boerner spotted it as he was walking through the gardens with W.I. Johnston of the McGredy firm, it reminded him of roses he had noticed in prints of early nineteenth-century scenes. Some of the blooms pictured were slate colored, and he had wondered if it was an artist's mistake. But perhaps this peculiar-looking flower was a throwback to a vanished strain. "I'll take some buds of that one," he said. Johnston protested. Who would want a gray rose? But the American insisted, and the Irishman finally said okay, "providing it's understood that it's none of my doing."

Back in Newark, Gene put the gray oddity through the usual testing pattern. It continued to please him in the company gardens, so he sent it to test plots around the country. The results were widely divergent. "A mistake," Salt Lake City reported. "A beautiful thing," said Lancaster, Pennsylvania. "The color is out of place among roses," Seattle claimed. "Cool and aloof — I would call it Serenity," Chicago countered.

So it was controversial, but what was so wrong with that? Boerner and Perkins agreed that a gray rose could find a place in the market. Now The Mouse needed a new name. A number of possibilities were considered and found wanting, until Helen Jepson visited the rose gardens. Charlie Perkins showed the rose to the Metropolitan Opera star, and Miss Jepson thought it was lovely; in fact, it just matched a string of pearls she had recently bought. "Why don't you name it Grey Pearl?" she asked.

Perkins passed the suggestion along to Boerner. He knew, in a

Jiminy Cricket, Floribunda (1954)

vague sort of way, that gray pearls were expensive, but he wasn't sure how expensive. The next time he was in New York, he hurried into Tiffany's. "I'd like to see some gray pearls," he told the salesman.

Gene was hot and disheveled. Thinking back on it afterward, he decided the man from Tiffany's took him for a shady character who might snatch up the pearls and dash down the street. But when he explained he was considering naming a rose for the pearls' gray shade, the salesman brought out a number of examples, among them a set of shirt studs the exact shade of the rose. Boerner hated to leave without buying something to repay the clerk for his trouble.

"How much for the studs?" he asked.

"Only thirty-six hundred dollars, sir."

Boerner decided to do without them, even if it meant being classed as a cheapskate by Tiffany's. But he was impressed. If people would pay thirty-six hundred dollars for shirt studs of that gray shade, surely they'd be willing to spend $3.00 or so to get a bush that would produce a summer-long crop. So The Mouse became the Grey Pearl, which went on to become an ancestor of Lavender Pinocchio, Amy Vanderbilt, and a number of other distinguished descendants.

As the 1950s progressed, Boerner was well on his way to becoming the most successful rose hybridist of all time. By the end of the decade he had a total of nine AARS winners; five more would be added to that list in the sixties. After Fashion and Vogue came Ma Perkins in 1953, Jiminy Cricket in 1955, White Bouquet in 1957, Gold Cup in 1958, and Ivory Fashion in 1959, all of them floribundas.

Jiminy Cricket was a cross between Geranium Red and Goldilocks in the hope of getting another coral-peach rose which would equal the success of Fashion. The result was a tangerine-red bloom which aroused almost universal approval when its tests had progressed to the point where it was shipped to the gardeners who helped Jackson & Perkins evaluate new roses. The list had grown to two hundred eighty-five and ranged from university trial fields to backyard gardens, including one tended by Gene's older brother, Arthur.

By the end of the 1952 season the rose was doing so well in the twenty-two test gardens used in the All-America Rose Selection trials that it seemed likely it would score high enough to win the AARS award. Boerner began to hunt for an appropriate name. The Walt Disney movie about Pinocchio was back in the theaters on one of its periodic revivals. The new rose was not a Pinocchio descendant, but why not name it for the insect which served as the wooden boy's conscience in the cartoon? Still mixing homespun show business with horticulture, Gene and the Perkins brothers prepared for the annual rose festival by planting a new Children's Storybook Garden in which a figure of Jiminy Cricket was surrounded by a large bed of the new Jiminy Cricket floribundas.

Geranium Red, the Boerner rose which was one of Jiminy Cricket's parents, was also the immediate ancestor of Spartan, whose other parent was Fashion. Introduced in 1955, the year Jiminy Cricket won its AARS title, Spartan became one of the most famous of Gene's roses, even though it failed to place high in the All-America competition. Spartan did well in tests held in most parts of the country; but its score in California, where the spring was cold and wet, pulled down its average.

The AARS award, it turned out, was one of the few honors Spartan failed to capture. The American Rose Society gave it a 9.3 rating out of a possible 10, the highest score yet attained by a floribunda, making it one of only eight roses that had rated nine points or better. Spartan won the Portland Gold Medal, the ARS's David Fuerstenberg prize, the NRS Gold Medal. But its failure to be chosen an All-America brought doubts about how heavily it should be propagated and promoted.

Boerner insisted that Spartan was worth pushing hard. Perkins agreed. The company spent $150,000 to introduce it, including a full-page advertisement in *Life* magazine. The promotion paid off. Spartan went on to become one of the biggest sellers in the catalogue and one of Gene's favorite roses for hybridizing. Other growers agreed on its usefulness as a parent; by the late 1950s, Boerner estimated, three out of every four new roses being developed in Europe made use of the Spartan strain.

The company's gambles on a new rose did not always turn out so happily. As Charlie Perkins said in discussing the hazards of the rose business, "guess wrong and you have bushes to burn." One wrong guess came in 1953, when the company introduced a floribunda named Siren, which had won an NRS Gold Medal. It was a lovely rose. The bushes were vigorous. It bloomed freely, producing scarlet blossoms all summer. Out went the catalogues. Back came the orders. But not many of them specified Siren. At the end of the season seventy-five thousand of its bushes had to be tossed on the annual bonfire. In retrospect, Perkins decided he knew the reason. "The public just didn't want a rose to look like a fire engine."

Chapter XV

Roses Become Big Business

Mardi Gras, one of Jackson & Perkins' 1953 introductions, was an example of how a rose hobbyist could come up with a winner. Prof. G.L. Jordan of the University of Illinois had discovered a red mutation in his garden. He sent a twig containing three eyes to Boerner, who was known around the school's floriculture department as one of its particularly-distinguished graduates. Gene budded the eyes on bushes in his greenhouse. The blooms that resulted resembled New Yorker, which Boerner considered the finest of the red roses he had created. Jordan's rose was put through the long testing process. Budded onto field stock, Mardi Gras grew vigorously, and the blooms were even more handsome than they had been indoors. The rose was added to the catalogue and proved a steady though not a spectacular seller. Royalty checks in four figures started wafting toward Champaign and the professor who had discovered a new rose and known what to do with it.

By the mid-fifties Jackson & Perkins was paying out about $250,000 a year in royalties to the originators of patented roses in Europe and the United States. In turn, other companies paid royalties for Boerner's patents, which had become one of the firm's major financial assets. As the world's largest rose grower, J. & P. paid out more royalties than it took in. But the income from roses created by Boerner was substantial. Even more substantial was the amount saved in royalty payments by selling Gene's roses to the company's customers. In a single year $330,000 would have had to be paid out if the bushes had been patented by someone else. "We can afford to gamble real money on research," Charlie Perkins told a writer from the *Saturday Evening Post*. "If we come up with a winner, we get it back fast."

Along with the extensive research program in Newark, where five greenhouses were now set aside for Boerner's hybridizing experiments and at least one hundred thousand plants were under observation at a time, the company also maintained a research program at Pleasanton, California, with a hybridizer named Dennison Morey in charge.

Perkins estimated that a rose like Gene's Golden Masterpiece, introduced in 1954, had cost $50,000 before the company got back a dime. The gestation period of this winner had begun in 1947, when Boerner crossed Mandalay with Golden Scepter. The former had large yellow blooms that grew on a plant that was small and weak. Golden Scepter, on the other hand, had a vigorous bush, but its flowers were nothing to brag about. If the cross resulted in a plant with Mandalay's spindly bush and Golden Scepter's undistinguished blossom, it would be a loser. But if the reverse were true — .

And so the cross was made, with Boerner gambling on the odds, and the plants that sprouted from the seeds were carefully studied. Most of them were worthless. But one grew into a sturdy bush that produced gorgeous yellow blossoms, seven inches across. "We've got a winner, Charlie," Gene told his boss. "Come out and have a look."

The two men studied the bush, arriving early while the dew was still on its leaves and the bloom was fresh as the dawn. They were old hands. They knew that before they could be sure, the new rose had to be tested and tested again. The process went on for five years. Finally, Boerner was satisfied. "You know, Charlie, this may turn out to be my masterpiece." The remark made the choice of a name easy, for once. "We'll call it Golden Masterpiece," Perkins said.

The hybrid tea had the long stems florists needed for bouquets for their cut-flower trade. In 1952, the company budded one hundred fifty thousand of the variety, planning to sell it mostly to professional growers. But they guessed wrong. The florists were satisfied with the yellow varieties they were accustomed to and saw no need for another one. But the home gardeners had a different reaction. They sent in so many orders that the new rose was soon blooming in gardens from coast to coast. The lottery conducted annually in the Newark greenhouses had turned up a winner again.

By the late fifties the wholesale portion of Jackson & Perkins' business had shrunk to twenty-five per cent of the annual total. There was more resistance in the wholesale market to the smaller-flowered floribundas than there was among gardeners, but some florists saw their advantages. Bouquets made from these roses might not be as spectacular as those using hybrid teas, but the floribundas lasted longer in steam-heated apartments without fading. Potted floribundas could also be sold as house plants, although they were not as popular for the Easter or Christmas trade as the improved strains of chrysanthemums, including a series named for birds which Boerner had created for Jackson & Perkins.

Golden Masterpiece, Hybrid Tea (1954)

Until a few years previous, mums were grown in greenhouses only in the fall. When hybridists produced strains which could be grown successfully throughout the year, this brought new competition for roses. Boerner set to work to produce greenhouse floribundas that would outlast hybrid teas and compete on a more even footing with chrysanthemums. By intensive cross-breeding, he lengthened the stems and gave the flowers higher crowns as well as adding a wider range of colors.

In part because of such constant efforts to improve its product, the company was prospering and expanding. When Boerner arrived in Newark, Jackson & Perkins had about a hundred employees. Now it employed two thousand. More than six hundred freight car loads of plants were kept in the company's storage cellars, awaiting shipment to customers. Besides the Newark acreage, the company had extensive holdings in Pleasanton and Newman, California, and near Phoenix, Arizona, as well as smaller properties in New Jersey, Delaware, and Indiana.

The Arizona and California operations were supervised by Clarence G. Perkins, who had joined the firm in 1911 at $7.00 a week. He had traveled as a salesman for twenty years before going to California in 1931 to take charge of the operations there. Jackson & Perkins Co. of California acquired a thousand acres at Pleasanton, another thousand in the San Joaquin Valley at Newman, but this was not enough. It added another thousand-acre plot in the desert near Phoenix.

Charlie Perkins passed his fiftieth anniversary with the company in 1952, but he continued to put in the kind of hours that had been customary when he was a twelve-year-old weed-puller. By 5 a.m. he was having breakfast. By 6 he was in the fields, often meeting Boerner there to inspect the test plots. The two often held another inspection at noon, when the hot sun would have had its effect, and a third in the evening.

Gene was content to use his own legs during these walks, but Perkins often rode his white horse, Silver. Up and down the rows he went, dismounting only when he wanted to take a closer look at a rose that struck his fancy. As a good rosarian, Silver took care not to trample the bushes.

Besides his duties in Newark, Boerner continued to spend considerable time traveling. The twelve months that ended July 1, 1952, were typical. In July, 1951, he spent a day in Washington, five days in New Orleans, then left for Europe, returning August 21. In September, he visited New York City and California. In October he spent three days in Tulsa, went to New York for a television appearance, back-tracked to

California for a rose meeting, and returned to Manhattan for a chrysanthemum show. November was comparatively quiet, with only a one-day
meeting in New York City tempting him to leave Newark, and in
December he also got no farther from home than Manhattan until it was
time for his annual Christmas pilgrimage to Wisconsin.

In January things picked up. There was a two-day meeting of
nurserymen in New York, a three-day nurserymen's gathering in Chicago, and two days at another meeting on the Cornell campus. In
February he lectured on roses in Milwaukee and Chicago. In March he
attended a garden meeting in Washington, flower shows in New York
and Boston.

April was a particularly busy time around Newark, and he avoided
out-of-town commitments; but by mid-May he had his work well enough
in hand to head for California and an inspection of the company's
operations there, then return to New York for the AARS presentations.
In June he made trips to Michigan and California, bringing the twelve-
month cycle to a close.

Boerner's complicated schedule reflected some of the complexities
of the business that was his livelihood. The days when raising and
selling roses was a leisurely sort of neighborhood occupation were long
since gone. During the 1950s total sales of nursery products had risen to
$650,000,000 in the United States, nearly double the total of ten years
before. Jackson & Perkins was riding the tide of this market expansion,
which coincided with the outpouring of city dwellers into what had
recently been country. By now, the company was spending $1,800,000 a
year on advertising and promotion, leading the way in a revolutionary
trend toward the mass marketing of rose bushes by mail. Its gross
income had climbed to $10,000,000 a year.

Most of the two million bushes it sold annually were bought by
catalogue customers. Occasionally, special promotions were held to seek
a new crop of buyers. These special deals involved sending roses to
gardeners who were not required to pay for them until the bushes
bloomed. This was a gamble. The finest bush might never bloom if the
gardener failed to to his part, and about one of each five such bushes
were never paid for. Still, the chance to attract new customers was
considered worth the expense.

Although the company was now a multimillion dollar business,
Nature showed it no special respect and precautions had to be taken. If
the weather turned frosty in late spring, a thermostat activated a bell in
the head gardener's house. This was the signal for him to leap out of bed

and begin phoning for reinforcements to save the roses. Everyone was expected to turn out, from Charlie Perkins to the newest apprentice. They brought with them smudge pots and kerosene stoves to put at strategic points, trying to keep the temperature from falling below freezing.

It was a makeshift system, and Perkins, among many others, wearied of it. By the late fifties he had installed huge blowers like those used in California orange groves. The bell still clanged in the head gardener's cottage, but now the company executives could stay asleep. The gardener simply turned on the fans which kept the air moving, and, if all went well, staved off the frost. The system was reasonably effective at the public rose garden, but the growing fields were too large for any such arrangement. The plants there had to take their chances. Frost could be expensive. In the spring of 1958, for example, the shoots were four or five inches long on the bushes when the weather changed and they were frozen. The company lost a quarter of a million roses overnight.

During the hard times of the thirties such a freeze had wiped out some smaller nurseries; the cost of insuring against such natural disasters was prohibitive. Largely because of such unfavorable weather, Jackson & Perkins found itself nearly a million dollars in debt at one stage of the Depression. The company fought its way back to solvency, but no one was likely to forget the dangers in dealing with a product that could be ruined by a late spring cold spell.

The weather also affected sales. A dry spring meant slow orders, as customers waited to see what was going to happen. A wet spring, on the other hand, meant business would boom. Unable to get out in their gardens because of the mud, rose fanciers had plenty of time to sit before the fire and look at all those wonderfully seductive photographs in the Jackson & Perkins catalogue.

Partly to seek a more favorable climate, J.& P. decided in 1954 to move a rose bed from Texas to Arizona, which sounds like a simple enough task except that the rose bed in question contained two million bushes. Charlie Perkins clamped down on his cigar and issued orders. A task force of digging machines fanned into the Texas field to uproot two million bushes. Workmen pruned them, loaded them in boxcars, and shipped them to Newark. The staff there stacked them in cold storage bins so they could stay dormant until it was time to package them in individual cartons and dispatch them to rose growers.

Meanwhile, new gardens near Phoenix were being prepared. The

Texas-sized rose bed had been big, certainly. But the new one was to be bigger. By the time all the cuttings had been planted in the sandy soil, the Arizona field contained not a mere two million rose bushes but ten million. Never in the history of the world had there been a garden that large. It was not the company's only rose garden, however. The ones in Newark now contained four million bushes, the ones in California had eight million, and there were smaller garden plots in Ohio, Oregon, and Delaware — not over five hundred thousand bushes in each, so hardly worth mentioning. In all, the company had about twenty million rose bushes; and as each bush was sold, another would be ready to take its place.

Machinery as well as skilled manpower was needed to produce roses on a scale never before attempted. In California and the new gardens in Arizona, mowing machines were used each October to top the millions of market-sized bushes eighteen inches above the ground. Then mechanical diggers uprooted the bushes, to be trimmed and shipped to Newark. Huge refrigerated warehouses were waiting there to store the bushes until they were ready to be packaged in cartons, their roots surrounded by damp moss or sawdust, so they could be dispatched to customers.

Most of the customers bought partly on faith, the conviction that the roses which grew in their gardens would be as lovely as those blooming so grandly in the slick paper catalogues which J.& P. used as its chief marketing tool. So many roses were being offered that the gardeners had trouble deciding which to buy. Many of them concentrated on present and past All-America winners, on the theory that these had been tested by experts and found outstanding. Selling AARS winners was fine, but in a volume operation it seemed necessary to widen the appeal of other J. & P. roses. The result was one of the most successful promotional methods the company ever undertook. As many as fifteen thousand gardeners bought roses at a bargain price, in return for which they were asked to send back reports on which of these new varieties they liked best. The one with the highest score was named Rose of the Year. An import, Kordes Perfecta, with creamy white petals edged with carmine, was the first year's winner. "This system proved to be immediately successful," Charlie Perkins reported. "Sales during the introductory year have eclipsed anything in previous experience. Instead of a few thousand plants as in the past, the public demand has resulted in first year sales in the hundreds of thousands."

In a typical year in the 1950s, Jackson & Perkins offered its customers a choice of one hundred forty-two varieties of roses, including twenty-six unpatented kinds. Of those still protected by patents, forty-five had been hybridized by Boerner. Most of the others were those he had brought back from one of his European scouting trips. Although he chose only the most promising specimens on such journeys, most did not prove worth marketing. It was part of Boerner's job as research director to make periodic reports to the Europeans on how their hybrids were faring in the United States. His reports aroused frequent disappointment and occasional hard feelings. But as experienced hybridizers, the Europeans generally understood that the standards had to be kept high and the ruthless weeding-out of less-successful bushes had to continue.

In one typical report Gene told Jean Gaujard that of seventy-four of the Frenchman's roses currently being tested by Jackson & Perkins, all but thirty had been eliminated for reasons such as these:

"Not enough petals."
"Flowers too floppy."
"Burns quickly."
"Too weedy."
"Weak neck."
"Color fades quickly."
"Flowers small and have no class."

Of the thirty which had survived the preliminary tests, Boerner had high praise for only one. Number 5699, he told Gaujard, was "particularly interesting," an evaluation that still did not commit him to anything but tempered the bad news with at least this one ray of hope for future royalties.

Even though he had to be the frequent bearer of ill tidings about their roses, Boerner remained friendly with his fellow hybridists across the ocean. Whenever one of them was in the United States, he usually headed at once for Newark, once he'd found it on a map. If the visitor and his family were sightseeing in America, one of the first sights they usually saw was Gene Boerner and the J. & P. rose fields.

Informed by Alex Dickson, Jr., that his daughter, Shirley, was staying with a family friend in New Jersey, Boerner at once dispatched a bouquet of roses, "just to show you that there are flowers in the world," and invited her to visit Newark. When she arrived, Gene dropped everything to give her and her friends a conducted tour, showing how the roses were dug, stored, and shipped so she could compare the American methods with those at her father's nursery in Ireland.

In 1953, Boerner was visiting a rose show in Hamburg when he learned that his old friend, Mathias Tantau, had died. Since the end of World War II, Tantau had been officially retired, turning over his nursery to his son, Mathias, Jr., but he had continued his hybridizing in a small greenhouse at his chalet in a private forest. The elder Tantau had been a close friend of Wilhelm Kordes, the hybridist with whom Boerner maintained the closest of his overseas friendships. Now a white-haired patriarch, the six-foot Kordes had been in the nursery business since he was a fourteen-year-old apprentice in 1905. World War I had caught him in England, where he was interned as an enemy alien until 1919, then went back home.

Mathias Tantau, Jr.

"I crossed the Dutch frontier into a land full of hunger, revolution, and strife," he said of that return to his homeland. "It was not the very best climate to grow roses in. Often it looked as if all work on beauty and roses was sheer nonsense, if not worse. However, I stuck to my work, and with Max Krause, who had also come to Holstein, and Mathias Tantau

Gene S. Boemer, Floribunda (1969)

we became a trio very much interested in our rose breeding and not troubling about the political devils all about."

Boerner always reserved a portion of his European trips for long conversations with Kordes, who had much the same attitude toward the rose and its development as he did. His 1957 trip was typical of how much he managed to crowd into these journeys. He flew to Hamburg on July 31, spent four days with Kordes and other German growers, then headed for Amsterdam and four days in Holland. By August 8 he was in Belgium. Next came a flight to Paris to catch the night train for San Remo and two days in Italy, then on to Corsica and back to Paris before going to England and Northern Ireland. He was back in New York on August 21.

As an internationally-famous hybridist, Boerner was made welcome. When he appeared at the International Rose Conference in London the following year, he was persuaded to make a speech. Actually, not much persuasion was needed, even though he could not start the talk by offering a free rose bush to anyone who could stump him with a question about roses as he often did with less-knowledgeable gatherings.

"I have been specializing in floribunda roses and that goes back to my youth in Wisconsin when all we had were hybrid perpetuals," Boerner said. "We used to go to twenty degrees below zero, and the few hybrid teas that were available in my youth were not hardy enough. Therefore, after I had gone into hybridizing one of my objectives was to create things that are hardy and beautiful so that the people in those climatic conditions can have as good roses as others in more favored conditions. I think we have succeeded....

"Spartan, which we feel is going to be one of the biggest-selling floribundas, is the result of a cross between Fashion and Geranium Red. Between the two I was trying to get a little more body into Fashion and some of the fragrance. Spartan has appeared and is fragrant and a good-growing rose. At the World's Fair in Brussels, at the foot of the flags outside the American Building, we had several thousand Spartans growing to a great height with immense flowers. There I might tell you a little secret — we have thirty per cent of peat moss added to the soil to get aeration and these roses grew."

Boerner described how he decided which crosses were worth keeping. "You get some seedlings and you say to yourself: 'My goodness, that is lovely.' But is the petal stiff? Is there fragrance? Does it keep its foliage? These are the requirements you must look for."

Boerner was accumulating honors in his own country as well as abroad. The American Rose Society awarded him its David Fuerstenberg Gold Medal, the ARS's highest award, for "improving the floribunda rose and increasing its popularity and usefulness." The Massachusetts Horticultural Society gave him its Jackson Dawson Medal for rose breeding. Kordes wrote to tell him he had been selected to honorary membership in the Verein Deutscher Rosenfreunde. Book publishers were interested in having him write about roses.

He was receptive to the suggestion and made some notes, but there never seemed to be enough spare time available to tackle such a time-consuming project. Besides, his health was no longer robust. In 1953, his doctor ordered him to take two months off and loaf in a warm climate. Obediently, Boerner went to the Virgin Islands in February to escape the New York winter. But he soon got restless. The thought of all that work waiting for him at home made it hard to enjoy the sand and sun. Besides, he missed his roses. By March he was back at work.

Several years later, he began spending some time each year in a hospital in Springfield, Illinois, to rest and recover his strength. His good friend, Prof. Pearson, had a physician son in the Illinois capital, so Gene put himself in the hands of Dr. Raymond F. Pearson. "The home doctors would be too soft on me," he explained. Dr. Pearson was tougher. Sometimes he ordered complete bed rest, which included a rule against having a telephone; otherwise, he knew, Boerner would spend too much time talking to Newark and accumulating worries about how things were faring there with him gone. Some years, Gene spent as many as three separate periods at the Springfield hospital. It was the only way he could relax and quit worrying about those ten thousand newborn floral children of his in the greenhouses and test gardens.

There was really no way anyone could keep him from working, however. He might have an assistant fly out with samples of roses or chrysanthemums that looked promising so he could decide which ones should be used in his next series of crosses. He dictated evaluations of his bedside roses into a recorder, sometimes murmuring into the microphone during those early morning hours when the hospital was quiet but he couldn't sleep.

His Uncle Albert had moved to Florida, with Gene helping out financially so a veterans' pension would stretch to cover the mortgage on a house there. Albert had arthritis, but he continued to dig in his garden and send back reports on the roses his favorite nephew sent him.

The family ranks were beginning to thin. Boerner's sister was widowed in 1952. Three years later, death came to Alfred Boerner. In 1958 Uncle Albert had a stroke that proved fatal. Gene began to take note of the chill breath of encroaching time. When he returned to Wisconsin for his 1959 Christmas visit, he was in a nostalgic mood. With his oldest brother Arthur he spent Christmas morning touring his boyhood haunts, reminiscing of nearly-forgotten times.

The brothers drove to Cedarburg. On the way they talked of some of the Teutonic nobility that had settled in the vicinity: a man who had not one but two vons in his name (von Zastrow von Kussow) but served in the somewhat lowlier station of county clerk; the woman who had once owned vast estates but lost them, came to America, and was best known around Cedarburg for the aromatic qualities of her goats. Then the talk turned to the Kümmel Kirche, a church named for a caraway-flavored liqueur admired by German settlers. The name went back to a Sunday when the pastor discovered to his dismay that he was out of Communion wine. Luckily, a parishioner had a full bottle of kümmel he was willing to donate to the good cause. It was substituted, giving the congregation a pleasant glow and the church a new name.

On his European travels Gene had formed the habit of using a tape recorder to preserve his thoughts and observations; and as he and Art rolled along in their car through the familiar countryside, he spoke into his recorder: "Here is an old apple orchard to my left in which the trees are just about gone. Undoubtedly that orchard was planted by one of the pioneers, but that terrible freeze in the thirties decimated a great many of these trees and gave them black heart and so forth.

"...We have just passed the site of the old Bonniwell house which, unfortunately, has fallen into decay....Bonniwell was, in his early days, a ship's carpenter and he had this house beautifully built and beautifully finished in the interior....We have just passed the old O'Brien homestead. George O'Brien was an old friend of mine and was in school with me. Their homestead is one of the stone houses that was built in the early days. We are now also passing the relics of some of the original fox farms. Here was the beginning of the raising of foxes in cages for the fur business.

"...We are entering Cedarburg from the west. This is my old stamping ground. We are passing through Cedarburg on the road to Five Corners, which had two things in my youth. One was the creamery, where the Boerner Brothers and father and Uncle Gustave were active stockholders and organizers. And the other was the Baby Hartwig's Saloon, which I can remember because we had pigeons in our woodshed and the Hartwigs would have pigeon shoots and we would bring our pigeons out there and sell them to Mr. Hartwig and the people who would shoot clay pigeons would then get these birds...."

The ride continued past a farm where Gene remembered the owner had been Patrick Halpin, a six-foot Irishman with "tousley" hair. They crossed the old covered bridge above Cedar Creek, the boards covered with carved initials, then passed a place where Gene remembered there had been a mill (Koehler's Mill) which had been the center of a small settlement. They drove by an octagonal schoolhouse, no longer in use, which he said he hoped would be preserved. Then they went back into Cedarburg past a factory which had made nails when he was a boy. The owner of the mill, he reminded Arthur, had been referred to as "Nagle John." On Columbia Street, they passed a house where Gene remembered going for cookies. He was glad to see that the iron fence dividing his boyhood home from the neighboring yard was still there. "The old shed which was there had been changed into a two-car garage, but the elaborate outhouse which was there is gone," he confided to the tape cassette. "I much regret to see that gone." The ride took them past a house once occupied by his school principal, Papa Lau, who was, Gene said, "short and fat, had a white beard and always smoked cigars so that his beard was always stained on that side. The smell of cigar hung over him, summer or winter."

Such visits to his old haunts helped him retain contact with his beginnings as well as giving him a chance to talk over old times with relatives he loved. Family members continued to visit him at the cobblestone house on Seneca Lake, with Mrs. Schlueter sometimes spending weeks at a time there now that she was widowed, helping run the establishment for her bachelor brother. Arthur Boerner was there when Kordes arrived for his 1958 visit. As a dedicated rose-grower, Art found much in common with the German hybridizer, and the two quickly became friends. Kordes gave him a copy of *Das Rosen Buch,* inscribing it with a wry quotation: "The roses were my life assignment. They are like the women — beautiful, sparkling and desirable. Only after one has them does one notice they also have thorns."

Kordes had arrived with his younger neighbor, Mathias Tantau, Jr., by way of Los Angeles. They flew from Copenhagen over Greenland into Canada, then to Winnipeg, where the plane was refueled before continuing to California. Gene met them in San Francisco, and soon they were inspecting Jackson & Perkins' California rose fields, a task that took three days of what Kordes later described as "much walking, up and down, all day long. It is a hard climate for the roses there," Kordes said. "By night and half the morning there are very cold fogs, then the sun breaks and temperatures rise by ten or even twenty centigrade in a few minutes. Everytime I see the films I took there I think of this sudden change from cool to hot."

Kordes concluded that the California fields were a good place to discover whether a rose was able to survive difficult growing conditions. He felt that the climate in Newark, which was more like that of Holstein, was better for rose-growing. "The few that survived these merciless trials are those that made Gene famous for his new roses," Kordes said. "Maybe he was in his time the only breeder in America who really tried to realize his dreams and ideals of new roses."

After the California visit the German hybridizers visited the fields near Phoenix and then went to Peoria, where the company was seeking to develop virus-free roses. Kordes considered the Arizona fields "a fine and foolproof land for production of rose plants." The desert was as flat as a table, the water had to be drawn up from four hundred feet below the surface, the sun was blazing, but the roses grew well. "It was a funny sight," Kordes said, "on the left hand, cactus and thorny shrubs; on the right hand, roses in full flower. There were two great drawbacks, Gene told me: the cost of water and the many miles of rail between Phoenix and Newark."

Walking through the test fields at Newark, Kordes was impressed by some of the roses, but he felt that others should be rooted out and burned at once. His policy was to get rid of any bush that did not show outstanding promise by the time it was two years old. Returning to the company offices, Kordes met Charlie Perkins.

"Find some outstanding bushes?"

"We did," Kordes told him. "There are some that must be carefully watched. But the others—we should go this afternoon and tear them up. No sense cultivating useless things."

To his surprise, this evaluation made Gene Boerner angry. He protested that it was too soon to decide whether those roses were unworthy. "I never felt before how Gene was absolutely tied up with his creations," Kordes said later. "He never understood why we got rid of all seedlings that did not look promising. He often remarked, 'I do not quite see that your way is right; I'm afraid a good many are killed before they can show what's in them.' " Then the two friends would argue, neither feeling that the other was right.

"When I started breeding about 1905," Kordes said, "every seedling was something holy and untouchable. Well, that changed quickly when the numbers became larger. It is a terrible handicap to have all those useless seedlings standing around and never have a clear field. There was always the great difference between Gene and me. He kept them for many years and we were just the opposite.

"He was so much 'married' to his new roses that he must have often felt sorry to leave out any of them because another had to take its place. J. & P. rigorously kept to one hundred varieties of new roses and for any new one, an older one had to go.

"In this respect, Gene was much more one of the old gardener types. In talking with him, the old and bygone roses always cropped up. But was not this the sound foundation from which Gene was able to raise such wonderful new types? Without his knowledge of the old he would have been without an inner lead to what he ultimately achieved."

It was true that Boerner developed a special affection for some of his roses. If one of his favorites did not quite qualify for mass production and dissemination through the catalogue, he tried to rescue a few of the bushes, planting them in a friend's garden or in one of the beds at Gene's Landing so that the rose would survive. Sometimes his stubborn unwillingness to give up on a rose too early paid off, as happened with a variety he brought back with him from the Alfred Cobley nursery in Leicester, England. "As I was hurrying through the greenhouse," he wrote Cobley in 1960, "I saw one very lovely flower about four inches in size, with quite a different color. I do not even remember the number, but I did want to tell you that it was a lovely and unusual thing."

Boerner ordered extensive tests of this rose that had caught his eye, but they were disappointing. The plants failed to thrive in the greenhouse, and it seemed that he had guessed wrong. But instead of ordering the bushes burned he waited. Late in the season of 1961 his patience paid off. "It suddenly snapped out of it," he wrote to Cobley, adding that he was ordering two thousand of the bushes be produced and that the rose be entered in the All-America trials.

Cobley was delighted. He had the consent of the Duke of Bedford to name the rose Woburn Abbey after the duke's ancestral home, he told Gene, and he was sure the variety would sell well in Britain. Meanwhile, the rose was patented in the United States, sent out for further tests, and finally put on the market in 1965. The supply quickly sold out. "I am certainly happy it turned out the way it has," Gene told Cobley, "because I have always been very much taken with it."

Roses Become Big Business

By now Boerner was seeking to produce roses with greater resistance to such plant ailments as blackspot and mildew, which meant that Spartan or its descendants were used in many of the crosses. "Spartan is, I think, the most resistant rose in circulation," he said. "It not only has a gay color, but its foliage stays on, right down to the ground, all through the year." By producing Spartan-derived hybrids in a full range of colors, he hoped to create a race of rose bushes that would require little spraying because "a carefree gardener will put in more roses if the roses will behave."

For greenhouse customers Garnette was the variety he used most in his hybridizing. In a 1961 notation he explained his reasoning: "Taking Garnette as a base, I have transmitted the stiffness of the petals to many other cut flowers. The chrysanthemum was competing with roses, and roses, as a whole, were losing out. By hybridizing and getting Golden Garnette and Tiara — a white Garnette — along with coral Garnettes and a pink Garnette, we have been able to reestablish the rose in the cut flower business and also give people roses in the floribunda class which will last at least a week or ten days.

"Now I am moving that same firmness of petal into hybrid teas and we will be coming out with hybrid tea roses which will last that same length of time. The crispness of the petal is being carried over very nicely. Since a thin petal will not withstand the sun and wind of summer, this new series of crosses is really going to be a terrific advance.

"I am also working the Spartan type into large flowers and working the crisp petals from the Garnette types into the Spartan seedlings. There is where we will be getting the longer-lasting, disease-resistant and insect-resistant roses." The knowledge that most of the roses being hybridized in Europe included his Spartan in their ancestry gave him parental pride and confirmed his belief that, by and large, the European hybridizers had good sense.

Asked by an editor of *Better Homes & Gardens* to name the roses which best demonstrated certain characteristics, Boerner chose Spartan for the disease resistance and abundant foliage categories and Americana for a "red variety that does not blue. If you take any of my reds, you will find they do not blue," he added. "It has been one of my obsessions to keep the blue out of the red — due, I think, to the fact that I had so much association with Better Times, which came so close to spoiling the rose business as a cut flower. You take the progeny of Chrysler Imperial and you will get the blue in them very quickly and I do not like it and do not want my name attached to anything like it." Continuing with his answers to the editor's questions, Boerner said that Diamond Jubilee and Kordes Perfecta were strains which passed on to their descendants the sturdy stem and neck which he sought in his hybridizing. "Unless a rose can stand up and look in your face, I am not interested in it at all and do not proceed with it in hybridizing."

In 1964 Boerner had his tenth AARS winner with Saratoga, a descendant of White Bouquet, his 1957 All-America winner and the first white rose ever to win that high honor. Saratoga was a floribunda with a Damask rose perfume. It was named in honor of Saratoga Springs, New York, which was blowing the bugles that year for the centennial of its race track. It included both Pinocchio and Garnette in its family tree. Gene had been seeking a white rose with stiffer petals, better able to resist wind and rain. He felt that Saratoga achieved that goal.

Another white rose introduced the same year was a hybrid tea which Boerner had considered naming for himself. When President Kennedy was assassinated in Dallas in the fall of 1963, he called it the John F. Kennedy instead, making it a living memorial to the dead president. Beds of the new rose were added to the President's Rose Garden, originally planted by Thomas Jefferson, and to the Jacqueline Kennedy Rose Garden, both at the White House. Thousands of bushes were donated to public gardens in all parts of the country, with special plantings at the World's Fair and a thousand plants at the New York Botanical Garden. The rose's ancestors included such Boerner winners as Ma Perkins, Fashion, and Diamond Jubilee.

Another notable introduction in the sixties was Mexicana, the result of a 1958 cross between Kordes Perfecta and an unnamed red seedling, the last in a series of crosses he made in seeking to achieve a perfect bi-color hybrid tea. He had begun with Rome Glory, a prolific bloomer, chosen in the hope that its descendants would inherit its vigor but improve on its fragrance and color. By crossing and recrossing, he obtained a red rose which he then crossed with a seedling of Peace and Golden Scepter. The likeliest of the seedlings which resulted from this union were crossed, in turn, with Kordes Perfecta to produce Mexicana. This new beauty reflected its diverse ancestry. Its dominant color was an intense red, but the flower's outer petals were white or ivory. Mexicana was chosen Rose of the Year in 1966 by the fifteen thousand home growers who were participating by then in the annual testing of unnamed Jackson & Perkins varieties.

John F. Kennedy, Hybrid Tea (1965)

Roses Become Big Business

Earlier in the decade Boerner had decided that the market could use a red rose which would be as handsome as his New Yorker but have a larger bush and larger flowers. He crossed New Yorker with an unnamed seedling of Poinsettia. The result was Americana, which grew three feet tall, had blooms nearly half a foot across, and was used to illustrate the cover of an issue of *Business Week*.

This publication did not ordinarily deal in horticultural matters, but that issue contained an article describing "a heady new era of mass production and mass marketing of roses." Americana shared the cover with Charlie Perkins, who was shown sniffing the flowers with the respect due the first rose variety ever to sell half a million bushes in its first year on the market. This remarkable total was a tribute to Americana's beauty and to Boerner's hybridizing skill; it was also an indication of how successfully Jackson & Perkins was competing for the gardeners' dollars.

Annual sales of nursery stock were running close to one billion dollars in the United States in 1961, with roses accounting for perhaps $150,000,000 of this total. The market was widely fragmented, with a thousand large and middle-sized firms in competition, along with numerous small ones. J. & P. was the largest, but its rose sales accounted for only .05% of the annual total. The figures indicated that those who were calling Jackson & Perkins the General Motors of the rose business were exaggerating. Still, it had reached the point where it could be said that its marketing and research techniques had revolutionized the industry. Its merchandising was aggressive. It had moved into credit selling; about 15% of its customers were now buying roses with no money down, agreeing to pay only after the bush put out green leaves in the garden. It was significant that a survey indicated that nine out of ten of these credit customers had never before bought roses. "We've barely touched the market," Boerner told the man from *Business Week*.

Perhaps so, but it wasn't from lack of trying. The catalogues were still going to two million homes, even though each cost the company thirty-five cents to print and distribute. The number of salesmen calling on wholesalers had increased to an even dozen. The advertising budget was impressive, and the company managed to get free advertising as well by such devices as tie-in sales.

The Perkins brothers and Boerner understood that they were selling not only roses but the satisfactions that a gardener feels when he knows he's planting the best bushes obtainable and the prestige that goes with being able to outdo his neighbors. Bargain-priced rose bushes were available at chain stores and supermarkets, but Jackson & Perkins' customers were persuaded that the extra cost was worthwhile.

A rose picked as an All-America winner was automatically prestigious, but the competition was keen for this honor. J. & P. had hedged its bets by also throwing its promotional skills behind other worthy roses. It had long been obvious that promotion was needed to sell roses in quantity. The company's sales statistics proved the point. In 1958, for example, J. & P. had introduced a fine rose with a likely name — Baby Blaze — but had given this new variety no promotional boost. The result was a disappointing sale of sixty-five hundred bushes. By comparison, its 1957 All-America winner, White Bouquet, had sold ninety-five thousand the first year and another All-America choice, Fusilier, a J. & P. rose fathered in California by Dennison Morey, topped one hundred thousand.

So Jackson & Perkins launched its Rose of the Year contest, the first winner of which was handicapped by bearing a name which had been retained only in deference to that old friend of the firm, Wilhelm Kordes. He had called one of his final triumphs Kordes Perfecta. Gene would have preferred a catchier name. Even so, as Rose of the Year, Kordes Perfecta sold one hundred sixty-nine thousand bushes the first year it was introduced, even though an extra fifty cents had been added to its price to pay for promotion costs.

In 1961 Rose of the Year was Gene's Americana, and the target for its first year's sale — half a million bushes — would have been considered wildly impossible a few years earlier. But the company had learned new techniques of selling roses, and before the spring buying season was over that goal had not only been met but surpassed. Such success did not come cheap. Total selling costs, including catalogues and brochures sent to customers, now amounted to about $2,700,000 a year. But Boerner and the other owners felt that the expense could be justified, especially in view of the need to meet the growing threat of chain store bargain bushes. As one means of meeting this cut-rate challenge, it was decided to expand the Rose of the Year program. The consumer panel was asked to make its choices for two years ahead, giving the company a chance to produce more stock and to organize its promotional activities for the winner well in advance.

If the fragmented competition made it impossible for one firm to dominate the market so J. & P. could fulfil the role of a General Motors, it might be more accurate to call the company the Cadillac of the rose business. Jackson & Perkins emphasized quality and prestige, with a touch of show business thrown in for good measure. From 1959 to 1960 the firm's total assets rose by nearly one-and-a-half million dollars to $13,500,000. Expansion had been steady since World War II, and there seemed no reason why it would not continue. But after 1960, the trend turned downward. By 1965 the asset value was back to the 1959 total of $12,100,000.

The land which the company had bought on the outskirts of Phoenix had been caught up in the city's expansion and was now too valuable to be used for roses. The Phoenix Farms Company, an Arizona corporation which owned the acreage, belonged to the Perkins brothers and Boerner; Gene owned a fifth of the stock in this subsidiary. When the land was sold and the Phoenix company's assets were liquidated in 1956, the proceeds were divided. Boerner more than doubled his original investment, but there were those who said later that it would have been better if the proceeds of the sale had been used to pay off some of the parent company's debts.

Another tract was purchased farther out in the Arizona desert. Of the forty-five hundred acres in the Harquahala Valley northwest of Phoenix, about eighteen hundred acres were needed for rose-growing, enough for three gardens of six hundred acres each. Each fall six hundred acres of bushes were dug, another six hundred acres of roses were left for the following year, and a third tract of six hundred acres was available for planting of bushes to be marketed two years hence.

The farm also contained an orange grove and cotton fields. It was hoped that these products would pay expenses, permitting the roses to be grown on the rest of the land at a profit. The acreage was thirty miles from the nearest railroad, however, and getting water for irrigation was expensive. The four-hundred-foot wells supplied enough water for the ranch to give every American seven gallons a year if it had been evenly divided among the citizenry. But lifting it to the surface and distributing it over the fields was costly. Boerner felt that he had not been sufficiently consulted before the Arizona move was made, and there were hard feelings among some of the company hierarchy.

There was another danger signal for those whose livelihood was tied up with the company's fortunes. The four men who had built it into the nation's largest mail-order nursery were getting old. "All four were at least in their sixties," one of Boerner's close friends said in describing that period in the company's affairs. "A man may be at his peak physically at thirty and at his peak mentally at forty, but the time comes when he starts to wane. And here were four men past sixty running the business. When Charlie died, the company had bank loans in Rochester, Elmira, various places, a big debt to carry. So a lot of the burden fell on Gene Boerner, and he was a better hybridizer than he was a businessman."

Charles H. Perkins' death came on March 6, 1963. On the surface, things went on as before. But the comfortable days when, as one associate put it, "Charlie ran the business and Gene did the hybridizing," were gone forever. "Charlie Perkins and Gene made that business," one of Boerner's friends said. "They made a marvelous team." But now Perkins was dead, and Boerner was tired and often ill. He had been hospitalized three times the year before and had worked only part time early in 1963.

In view of his age, Perkins' death should not have been totally unexpected. Boerner and the other three owners had discussed an orderly method of handing down the business to the next generation some years before. A variety of plans was talked about but nothing very effective was done, and the death of the firm's president and majority stockholder plunged Jackson & Perkins into a financial crisis.

Boerner shouldered an increased share of the burden of operating the business, including accepting the title of vice-president, but he continued to concentrate much of his energy on his hybridizing. The research program was a major asset of the company and could not be allowed to deteriorate. Of the company's three hundred eighty-three patents, about two hundred were still active, bringing in roughly $400,000 a year in royalties paid by other growers. Between 1953 and 1959 Jackson & Perkins had earned nearly a million dollars, after taxes. But if the $2,377,000 paid to the firm in royalties, mostly on Boerner's patents, had been subtracted, the nursery would have been operating at a loss. Only the hybridizing income had kept its operations in the black even during the period of its greatest prosperity.

The 1963 rose festival was scheduled only three months after Perkins' death, but it was decided to go ahead with the plans. The rose garden was renamed in his honor. Also honored that year were Boerner and Mathias Tantau, Jr., whose Tropicana had been chosen Rose of the Year by those thousands of customers who tested new roses for the company and paid for the privilege of doing so. One of the featured roses at the festival was a Boerner creation he called Junior Miss. Naturally, that meant that the 1963 Junior Miss, Diane Sawyer of Louisville, must be on hand. Among other visitors was Hermann Kordes, representing German hybridizers.

As before, the festival was a mixture of horticulture and show business. Seven-year-old Katherine Kemp was chosen Rose Princess, which gave her the duty of officially opening the festivities. There was a fashion show staged by a Rochester department store, a concert by bagpipers called the Genesee Highlanders, a picture-taking session organized by Eastman Kodak. That was on the first day. On the next, forty-five girl ballet dancers from Rochester, the Distaffettes, performed among the roses. Later came such events as the annual Sterling Bowl tournament, when flower arrangers competed for a trophy. There had been no serious thought of calling off the festival. It was important that the company's operations go forward unchanged. Rumors were already circulating in Newark that it would be sold, but these were denied as efforts were made to surmount the crisis that Charlie Perkins' death had brought to a head.

Even before, Boerner had sometimes told visitors: "Everything starts with me, you know." There were those who regarded such a remark as evidence of egotism. Still, in at least one sense it was no more than the truth; without his roses, the rest of the operation would have had little purpose. But he also took responsibility for numerous tasks that had little to do with hybridizing. William Zombory, a Detroit hybridizer, and his wife, Sophia, described him as a "human dynamo" as he sat in his luxurious office with its cork floor, bouquets of roses on his desk, a sign reading, "Genius At Work," above him. He would be "talking cross-country on the phone in his booming voice, looking over important papers, consulting with his secretary — his 'right-hand man,' without whom he would have been lost — or with his perennial man, Louis Ippolito or others, perhaps measuring the potential of a rose in his hand, all at the same time."

Discussing how he judged roses — his own or others' — that were being grown in the test fields, he told the Zomborys: "I never know whose rose it is, or what number. A rose must hit me in the face when I go down those rows. Otherwise, I go by it."

"Gene was a fair man," Mrs. Zombory said. "He was the first to admit when someone else's rose on trial was better than his own. One day we brought down from the fields one of our roses that was on test. He reached for the phone and had his greenhouse man send up a rose of his of similar color for comparison. He studied both roses carefully, smelling them, feeling them. Then he announced: 'Yours is better than ours'."

By 1963 visitors who dropped by his office found Boerner changed. When he spoke of roses the old enthusiasm remained. But he was no longer able to put in the long hours under the pressure of multiple duties that had once been routine. "I can see you only for a short time," he would say, regretfully. "Doctor's orders."

Despite his failing health, Boerner continued his regular visits to Europe. He went to Rotterdam early in 1963 to show his greenhouse roses, hybridized from the Garnette strain. But his old friend, Wilhelm Kordes, persuaded him to take the next flight home. He had recently left the hospital. It was plain that he was not well enough to do the things he had wanted to, and Kordes was relieved to see him climb back aboard the plane and head westward agan.

In July, however, Boerner was in Europe once more. He was the opening speaker at an international horticultural exposition in Hamburg, addressing fifteen hundred persons in the German language he had learned as a boy. He seemed to have regained his strength. Kordes said afterward that the week of the Hamburg show was one of the happiest times his American friend had spent in Germany.

When he was back home again, however, Boerner had to admit he was no longer able to follow his old routine. He was seventy now, and it was growing increasingly plain that no man goes forever. His brother, Herman, had died three years earlier of a heart attack while on his way home from a football game. Gene feared the same abrupt ending could be his unless he slowed down. He had inherited Uncle Albert's house in Fort Lauderdale, and he spent some of his time there. At Gene's Landing he had a chair lift installed so he could still enjoy the view of the lake from his second floor bedroom without having to climb the stairs.

He no longer felt able to make the rounds of the Newark test gardens on foot, but luckily this problem had been foreseen a few years before. What he called his portable office had been built. Two metal arms were welded to the front of a tractor. A deck was mounted on them. Perched on the platform as a workman drove the tractor slowly up and down the rows, Boerner was still able to inspect his roses. There were times when even riding in his portable office was beyond this strength, however. During part of one hybridizing season, he told Mrs. Pullen: "Margaret, I'm not up to it just now. You've been working with me so long, just go ahead and do what you know I want to do."

And so she did, making the crosses she believed he would have ordered if he'd been there. Some years later, when it no longer mattered whether the secret was told, she described the result: "I got White

White Masterpiece, Hybrid Tea (1969)

Masterpiece for him. I babied that seedling. Mr. Perkins asked how we were doing without Mr. Gene around, and I told him Gene had made out a list of crosses before he got sick. If he was able to work at all, he was always thinking about those greenhouses. One time he called me up from Florida and talked to me for two hours straight. All I could think of was the phone bill."

With Charlie Perkins gone, Boerner found himself worrying more and more about the business end of the enterprise. On his trips he sat in lonely hotel rooms scribbling notes to himself that indicate some of the turmoil of those days: "Company is its own worst competitor.... If we can do the job right, we can have the business.... Further research needed to get more data on wholesale level." Presumably thinking of the atmosphere around company headquarters after Perkins' death, he went on to say that "we were like a lot of chickens with their heads cut off — no policies and no ideas of what the requirements were to run such a business."

He feared that the Rose of the Year competition was being weakened by sending out plants that were not up to the company's traditionally high standards: "Poor plants. Lack of respect for customers as anything but someone to get money from. No pride in plants delivered. No attempts at quality control. No long range thinking. No coordination of sales promotions and stock. Very bad substitutions which led to disgruntlement among knowing customers. Who are we selling? The knowledgeable? Dumb bells? Too early preparation of sales promotion material without due respect for stock available. Too much credit sales. Too little cash sales. Tying up money. Sell Arizona farms? Move to California?"

At a time in his life when he should be able to relax and enjoy the success he had won, he was facing the loss of everything. If the company went under it would not only be a financial disaster, but what would happen to his roses? For that matter, what would happen to the carefully-accumulated knowledge of a lifetime on ways to improve flowers, making them more beautiful, more disease-free, less subject to insect and climatic perils?

Once again he considered writing a book to tell what he had learned about hybridizing. On an early fall day in 1965 he sat on the porch of his house at Gene's Landing with a writer for a women's magazine, seeking advice on how to put such a book together. One thing he wanted to discuss in such a book, Boerner said, was the development of different strains of roses. "For instance, the Pinocchio strain that left its pink at the end; the Spartan strain, which left the foliage down to the ground. Each one could be taken from scratch and brought up through." And then he added something that hints at his attitude toward the relationship between his life and his roses: "In themselves, they could almost be a picture of 'Papa Floribunda.'"

Perhaps he could describe how the qualities of certain rose strains had been worked into the hybrid tea crosses as well as the floribundas, he said. The advantages of such floribundas as Spartan had been used to counterbalance the anemic qualities of the hybrid teas. In fact, he went on, the floribunda and hybrid tea lines were converging to the point where they resembled a common type, with this trend influenced by the floribundas' ability to produce greenhouse cut flowers. There had been a time, he said, when greenhouse floribundas had produced nearly all their blooms at once, which was no good for a commercial florist. "However, by watching the hybridizing, you develop sixty or seventy flowers in a year off a floribunda, as cut flowers."

Boerner wanted to be able to discuss such things in his book. But perhaps it was not yet time to write it. After all, he was only seventy-two years old and still in his prime as a hybridizer. "I don't know that it's time for me to stop my work and write a book, or whether I can sit out here on the porch and write the book on hot days."

The other man suggested that producing a book was not that easy — "it is a pretty full-time thing." Gene agreed that this was probably so, even though Dr. Nicolas had turned out two volumes while he was heading the company's hybridizing program. "Nickie needed protection while he was writing his books," he said. "So I did the things that Nickie was supposed to be doing in the greenhouses — hybridizing and everything else — and nobody ever knew about it. Unfortunately, I don't have anybody that would cover for me."

And so the book never got written because there was always too much else to do. There were days when he still felt able to work long hours, carrying forward his hybridizing, and even on his less vigorous days the roses were never far from his thoughts. There was a difference now that he did not have a reputation to make but a reputation to protect. He was the dean, the old master, the champ. One magazine called him hybridizing's equivalent of baseball's Babe Ruth. He was getting used to being called flattering things. He was "the Henry Ford of the rose business," according to one writer, the "Nobel Prize winner of the world of roses," according to another. He was "Mr. Floribunda" or

Apricot Nectar, Floribunda (1965)

"the Father of the Floribunda" or, more informally, "Papa Floribunda," the designation he liked best.

When the New York State Nurserymen's Association elected him to its Hall of Fame, he listened to the associaton president, Bernard Stangler, declare that "no other man in history has had so much influence and as many roses patented under his name," with Boerner's patented varieties reading like "an honor roll in the history of modern roses."

"Seek the challenge of perfection," Gene advised the nurserymen when it was time to make his response. He went on to tell them: "...The old way is not good enough. We must constantly seek out and insist on a new and better way.... We not only will enrich our own lives but we will continue to improve the land in which we live. We will transform the barren into the beautiful."

His successful efforts to transform the barren into the beautiful also won him the annual gold medal award of the Men's Garden Clubs of America for outstanding achievement in horticulture to go with all the other honors he had accumulated. But he was more interested in the awards that went to his roses, and in 1966, when he was seventy-three, two more of them came through. Mexicana was named Rose of the Year, and Apricot Nectar became his eleventh AARS winner.

Despite his failing health, he attended the thirty-fifth annual rose festival that year to accept plaques from Cornell University and from *Flower and Garden Magazine* for his accomplishments in developing some one hundred fifty new roses, eighty chrysanthemums, and a variety of other perennials. It was said that any gardener with as few as half a dozen hybrid roses in his yard was likely, by the law of averages, to have at least one of Gene's creations among them. He had no way of knowing how many of those varieties still being tested would prove outstanding, but he had his customary high hopes for some of them. At least three of the roses being tested would go on to win All-America honors, it turned out, giving him a total of fourteen AARS winners, a mark for future pollenizers to envy.

In presenting Boerner with the Cornell award that summer of 1966, Dean Charles E. Palm of the New York State College of Agriculture praised his cooperation in Cornell's research, teaching, and extension program, and the citation noted his "pioneering work with the flori-bunda rose, which has not only helped to strengthen a growing florist industry but also contributed to a more beautiful America." Such personal honors were pleasant enough. But he felt that they couldn't compare to another advantage of the work he had chosen. "There is nothing more rewarding," he said, "than watching a seedling develop into an award-winning rose."

New Boerner roses continued to reach the market, some of them bearing the highest honors. The royalty payments for his patents continued to arrive at the company's treasury. The catalogues continued to appear regularly in two million mail boxes from California to Maine, each one containing the kind of art that was as appealing to a rosarian as a *Playboy* centerfold to a college boy.

But beneath this prosperous facade the company was in serious trouble. Along with everything else, the weather conspired against it. The 1964 growing season was unusually dry throughout the northeastern states. Gardeners were discouraged from ordering new roses. By 1965 annual sales had declined by nearly a million dollars, with wholesale orders dropping even faster than retail sales. The net loss for the fiscal year ending June 30 was about half a million dollars, compared with a profit of more than a quarter of a million dollars during the previous twelve months.

The company valued its land and facilities, together with its roses and other nursery stock, at about twelve million dollars. But J. & P. owed several million to various banks, and the bankers were not as confident of the safety of their investment as they had been when the firm was in the black and Charlie Perkins was running things. Besides, there was the question of what to do about Perkins' estate. Of 6,334 outstanding shares of stock, he had owned 3,200, with Gene holding 766, Mr. and Mrs. Ralph Perkins another 766, and Clarence Perkins having 1,602. There seemed to be no way to meet the obligations of Charlie's estate without taking some drastic action to solve the company's financial troubles. There was talk of a partial liquidation, with Boerner and the other minority stockholders taking the company's holdings in Illinois, New Jersey, and Indiana as their share. But the bankers refused to give up this portion of their collateral.

Meanwhile, Boerner had been told by his physician that his heart was enlarged, and "you are in low grade chronic heart failure." Such a diagnosis forced him to try to change his routine still further. It had been his custom to break off work each morning, jump in his Cadillac, and head for the small nearby community of Phelps for a second cup of coffee and a doughnut at 9 a.m. But now coffee was forbidden. So were doughnuts. He must watch his diet very carefully, he was told.

He tried to obey the warning. But at 9 a.m., the old habit reasserted itself. On some mornings Mae Lunay would see him sneaking down the hall to where the coffee pot was kept, looking for all the world like a small boy about to raid the refrigerator. Glancing around to see if he was observed, he would fill his cup, and then, to go with the coffee, he would snitch a cookie. If he caught his secretary looking at him, he would grin and tell her she should order him nothing but cottage cheese for lunch to make up for his sinful indulgence.

The visits to the Springfield hospital and the bed rest prescribed by Dr. Pearson were designed in part to keep him from working, but things seldom turned out that way. He continued to lie awake in his hospital room, letting thoughts flow into the tape recorder. "It is five o'clock on Thanksgiving morning," he confided to the microphone during a 1965 visit. "The air is absolutely calm, and the only thing that seems to have any motion to it is the smell of pancakes which has come over here from the kitchen, which is many blocks away.... Now I am in absolute peace and quiet on Thanksgiving morning in 1965, which I hope will portend a similar year.... We are looking forward to the coming year as a peaceful year, with much less daily mundane things to do and the regular instructive hybridizing to do, which will go on for a few more years."

But his recorded comments were more typically about the roses sent to him from Newark for his evaluation: "I think we have got a humdinger in Coral Princess.... Golden Wave Sport is an orange which is not going to go very far.... Ole is a red, about three inches; the flower has a tendency to curve the petals when it is opening and will not be important.... Lady Bird is a very small orange, shiny foliage, stiff-petaled, but I don't think it will catch hold.... Forever Yours is opening up beautifully, the color is very good, it has a lot of petals and is going to be a great rose.... H-6365, I think is the best prospect the competitors have. It is a red, very good form, good nose, keeps well, opens slowly, and it is something that we must watch because it is going to compete with our red floribunda.... H-9142 is a long-stemmed pink which flowers confused as it opens. I don't think that will bother us very much.... Meanwhile, the night nurse looks at me kind of funny. But she is very nice about it."

During 1966 he spent more time at the Clifton Spring (N.Y.) Sanitarium than at home. The food was good there, the service attentive, the atmosphere more pleasant than in a more modern hospital. Most important, Clifton Springs was close enough to Newark so he didn't feel out of touch with the things as he did in Springfield. At the company, the situation was building up toward a climax. Gene no longer felt able to handle his financial affairs by himself and he enlisted the help of a nephew, Roger Boerner, a Milwaukee attorney, to protect his interests.

By now prospective bidders for the firm had narrowed down to only one, a company in Medford, Oregon, called Harry and David. Its Bear Creek Orchards had been selling fruit and other items by mail ever since the 1930s Depression, when it had followed a pattern similar to Jackson & Perkins and had gone from wholesaling to the retail field. It had developed into a prosperous national operation, shipping more than a million orders a year to customers who wanted fancy foodstuffs.

The dickering over price went on for months, with the J. & P. representatives pointing out that their mail-order business would complement the Harry and David line and claiming that consolidation of the two companies would produce an annual sales volume of over twenty million dollars. Finally, late in June, 1966, the deal was consummated.

All outstanding stock in Jackson & Perkins was purchased for about $3,250,000, with Charlie Perkins' estate and the minority stockholders sharing in the proceeds. The terms specified that Eugene S. Boerner, recognized as one of the firm's prime assets, was to continue with the company, with J. & P. operating under its own name as a wholly-owned subsidiary.

The solution to the company's problems left Boerner with mixed feelings. He would have preferred that things somehow be restored to the conditions that had prevailed a few years back, with someone like Charlie Perkins around to handle most of the business worries and Gene free to concentrate on his roses. But it had long been obvious to him that those good old days had vanished forever and that, unless a suitable buyer could be found, the name of Jackson & Perkins might disappear, along with its traditions. If that happened, he had wondered, what would happen to his flowers?

Some of them would be safe enough. Even without a Jackson & Perkins Company gardeners would continue to grow those products of his hybridizing talents which had by now become old favorites. But what about all the others that were still being tested, those improved strains he hoped to have ready for the market next year and for several years after that? If the company simply disappeared, so would this legacy.

And so when Harry and David took over the company, there was a sense of relief for Boerner, mingled with his disappointment at how

First Prize, Hybrid Tea (1970)

quickly the old and comfortable ways had disappeared during the three years since Charlie Perkins' death. His financial assets had declined alarmingly along with the company's, but he could take comfort from the fact that the sale meant the company was still alive and well and that the future of his roses was still assured. Those promising floral children, the ones not yet ready to market, the ones he was still testing, would not be orphaned and abandoned, after all. The new ownership meant that Jackson & Perkins would continue to serve its customers as before. But there were changes in its operations. Under Harry and David's management the Arizona acreage was phased out of rose production in favor of a California location in Kern County, the same county where J. & P. had pioneered in West Coast rose-growing in the early 1900s.

Jackson & Perkins' traditional but inefficient method of sending millions of plants from its western fields to Newark, then reshipping them to customers, was abandoned. Beginning with the 1970 growing season, the plants were all shipped from Oregon, where J. & P.'s shipping, administrative, and research facilities were consolidated at the Harry and David headquarters in Medford. The company prospered under its new ownership. Those handsome catalogues continued to go out to customers, and for years to come Boerner's roses were among those featured in the lifelike photographs that set gardeners to dreaming of triumphs to come.

With the company's operations consolidated on the West Coast, it meant the end of the old ways in Newark. Wistfully, that little city continued to call itself the nation's rose capital. The rose garden found new owners and remained. Visitors continued to make pilgrimages to see its beauty. But an era had ended. The greenhouses and processing rooms on Newark's Madison Street were abandoned. The main office building was sold. The fifteen hundred acres of rose fields and farms were put to other uses.

It was during this period of transition that Boerner decided to sell the herd of prize cattle he had accumulated at Gene's Landing. He had put considerable thought and not a little hard cash into the herd, which now totaled ninety head. But he told his nephew, Roger, that it was time for it to be dispersed and asked him to arrange for an auction.

Gene had been in and out of the hospital no less than six times during that year of 1966. Each time, when he left Newark, his colleagues wondered if he would be back. Each time he fought his way to the point where he was permitted to leave Clifton Springs and return to his hybridizing. Mrs. Lunay had a theory about why he was so persistent: "He wanted to go with his shoes on."

His seventh trip to Clifton Springs was his last. On September 3, Margaret Pullen took a selection of new roses to his hospital room, as she had done so many times before. As was also customary, when Mae Lunay came he dictated his comments on each. Two days later he died. His body was taken home to the Boerner family plot in Cedarburg.

One of the legacies he left was an endowment to Cornell to be used to support rose research. But his principal legacy was left to the world's gardeners in the form of an unprecedented list of improved roses, ranging alphabetically from Aloha to Zorina. And even after death the list continued to grow.

Under its new ownership, Jackson & Perkins continued to regard the Boerner roses as one of its principal assets and to market and promote them accordingly. Other hybridizers took up the task of seeking new varieties, but additional varieties he had created continued to reach the market for at least a half dozen years after his death. Gay Princess was an AARS winner in 1967. The following year, he had another posthumous All-America rose in the pink floribunda which had been named the Gene Boerner in his honor. Then, in 1970, his First Prize was the only entry the judges considered worthy of the All-America rating. His work continued to bear fruit in 1972, when the season's new varieties included Aperitif, White Masterpiece, and Faberge, all of which he had created in those difficult but still productive months of hybridizing near the end of his long career.

A portion of the Newark rose garden was dedicated to his memory, with Reimer Kordes traveling to America to join in the ceremonies for his father's old friend. There was another less obvious posthumous memorial, the fact that no one who had known him well could ever pick a rose or walk through a rose garden without at least a fleeting thought of a man who had looked on such flowers as his children. His friends found his last Christmas message to be particularly appropriate. It was taken from "Song of Life" by Sean O'Casey: "I have found life an enjoyable, enchanting, active and sometimes terrifying experience and I've enjoyed it completely. A lament in one ear, maybe, but always a song in the other."

Bump Howard, the newspaperman who had helped him pick those annual Christmas messages, had reminisced with Boerner at the hospital at a time when it was obvious the great hybridist's life was ending. "When you think of all the roses and other flowers you've developed,"

Howard said, "it must give you a lot of satisfaction."

Once Gene might have shrugged off such a remark or changed the conversation to talk of roses of the future instead of those of the past. But now he could admit to a feeling that might have seemed overly-sentimental in the normal course of masculine talk. His words were a summation and an epitaph for a career: "Bump, you can't realize the satisfaction it gives me now to know that all those little children of mine — all over the world — will be pushing up their heads when I'm gone."

BIBLIOGRAPHY

Papers and Documents

Eugene S. Boerner. Letters to and from, various dates (in custody of Roger L. Boerner, Milwaukee).

Eugene S. Boerner. Papers and photographs (in custody of Roger L. Boerner, Milwaukee).

Eugene S. Boerner Papers. Collections #2639 and 2831. Cornell University Archives.

Boerner Family Genealogy (manuscript) (in custody of Roger L. Boerner, Milwaukee).

Catalogue of Cedar Hedge Farm Association. Cedarburg, Wis., n. d.

Information Kit about the Jackson & Perkins Company (typescript). Newark, N. Y., n. d.

Jackson & Perkins Research Program. Geneva, N. Y.: Jackson & Perkins, 1960.

Luther v. C. J. Luther Co., December 20, 1902-May 29, 1903. 118 Wisconsin, 112-119; 94NW69.

Minutes, Board of Directors, Jackson & Perkins Co., March 2, 1965 (typescript).

Books and Articles

"All-America Rose Selections Award Winning Rose for 1970." *The American Rose* 20 (June 1969): 2.

"Bachelor Rose-Grower Adds to National Honors." *Rochester Times-Union* June 23, 1966.

"Bird Chrysanthemums a Memorial to Boerner." *Asbury Park Sunday Press,* January 8, 1967.

Boerner, Arthur R. "German Pioneer Letters." *Wisconsin Magazine of History* 16 (June 1933): 428-48.

Boerner, Eugene S. "All American Rose Selections." *House and Garden* (October 1940).

Boerner, Eugene S. "Modern Roses for Modern Gardens." *The Gardener* (September 1962): 17.

Boerner, Theodore A. *C. Friedrich Boerner.* Cedarburg, Wis.: Privately Printed, 1937.

"Boerner Wins More Honors." *Milwaukee Journal,* July 3, 1966.

"Cedarburg Recipes in 'House Beautiful'." *Cedarburg News,* December 14, 1940.

Cherdron, Eliza Taylor. "Cedar Hedge Farm — In Retrospect." *Cedarburg News,* September 17, 1941.

Cunnion, Dan. "Roses That Can Rough It." *Farm Journal* 81 (June 1957): 86-87, 142-43.

Derwig, George. "Genie with Green Thumb Has Magic Golden Touch." *Illinois State Register* (Springfield), Oct. 18, 1963.

"Developer of Prize Rose Has Roots in Wisconsin." *Milwaukee Sentinel,* June 8, 1963.

Dickson, Alexander. "Obituary: Eugene S. Boerner." *The Rose Annual* (of the Royal National Rose Society, England) (1967): 147.

"Eugene S. Boerner." *The Rose* 15 (Autumn 1966): 36-37.

"E. S. Boerner Dies; Famous Rose Expert." *Milwaukee Journal,* September 8, 1966.

"Eugene Boerner, Rose Hybridizer." *New York Times,* September 7, 1966.

"Festival Opens in World Famous J & P Rose Garden." *Newark (N.Y.) Courier-Gazette,* June 14, 1962.

"Gene Boerner, Noted Rosarian, Dies on Monday." *Newark (N.Y.) Courier-Gazette,* September 8, 1966.

The Growth of Half a Century, 1874-1924. Newark, N. Y.: Jackson & Perkins Co., 1924.

"How a Rose Grower Keeps the Bloom in Profits." *Business Week,* No. 1648 (April 1, 1961): 54-58.

Johnston, J. W. "Rose in All Its Glory at Upstate Festival." *New York Herald Tribune,* June 26, 1955.

"J-P Dedicates Memorial Rose Garden Saturday." *Newark (N.Y.) Courier-Gazette,* June 29, 1969.

Keiper, Elizabeth. "Pre-Spring Question: What Was Winter Toll?" *Rochester Times-Union,* March 15, 1963.

Keiper, Elizabeth. "The World of Roses Is Ever-Changing." *Rochester Times-Union,* June 21, 1968.

Kinkead, Katharine T. "A Rose Is a Rose Is a Business." *New Yorker* 34 (July 19, 1958): 37-67.

Kozelka, Art. "E. S. Boerner, Dean of Rose Hybridists." *Chicago Tribune,* March 15, 1964.

Kozelka, Art. "40,000 Roses in One Garden." *Chicago Tribune,* July 19, 1964.

Kozelka, Art. "New Tea Rose to be Named for Kennedy." *Chicago Tribune,* December 27, 1964.

Kozelka, Art. "Rose Hybridizers Make It a Habit." *Chicago Tribune,* June 6, 1966.

"Letter from Wilhelm Kordes, Sparrieshoop, Germany." *New York Times,* January 10, 1960.

"Likens Roses to Auto Sales." *Milwaukee Journal,* June 21, 1957.

McDade, Matt C. "New York State's New Main Street." *National Geo graphic Magazine,* 110 (November 1956): 567-618.

"Man Behind the Plant." *Los Angeles Times,* January 19, 1964.

"The Million-Dollar Rose." *This Week Magazine,* September 26, 1954.

"Obituary for Mr. E. S. Boerner." *The Sea of Roses* (1967): 27 (in Japanese)

"Obituary to Our Honored and Beloved Rosarian and Hybridizer." *Soutl Carolina Rose Society News Letter* (November-December 1966): 5-6.

"Old Ozaukee Christmas Recipes Reprinted in National Magazine." *Por Washington Herald,* December 11, 1940.

"Personalities in the Plant World: Meet Eugene S. Boerner." *Flower anc Garden* 10 (June 1966): 29, 45.

Rosa Americana. "Rose-buying Spree." *Christian Science Monitor Weekl: Magazine Section,* June 3, 1944.

"...A Rose by Another Name." *Oilways,* 26 (September 1960): 1-5.

"Rose Hybridizer Speaks at Cornell Meeting." *Flower News,* December 26 1964.

"Rosen in Frankfurt und eine Rose Namens 'Frankfurt'." *Mitteilung de: Stadtverwaltung Frankfurt A. M.,* 16 Dezember 1961.

"Roses 1967." *Horticulture* 44 (July 1966): 32-33.

Stevenson, Tom. "The John F. Kennedy Rose." *Washington Post Potoma((March 14, 1965): 16-17.

Taylor, Frank J. "The Great Rose Lottery." *Saturday Evening Post 23" (February 26, 1966).

"A Tribute to Eugene S. Boerner." *American Rose Annual* (1967): 47-48

"Two Roses Receive AARS Title." *Milwaukee Sentinel,* June 8, 1963.

Van Ryzin, Gerald S. "Magical and Charismatic Roses." *Milwaukee Jour nal,* June 5, 1977.

Witte, Oliver R. "All-America Roses." *Milwaukee Journal,* May 26, 1968

"A Word from the President: Tribute to Eugene Boerner." *ARS Annua, (1967): 11.

Appendix

Eugene S. Boerner's All-America winners in the annual AARS competition to choose the season's best rose or roses were:

Katherine T. Marshall (HT) 1944
Diamond Jubilee (HT) 1948
Fashion (F) 1950
Vogue (F) 1952
Ma Perkins (F) 1953
Jiminy Cricket (F) 1955
White Bouquet (F) 1957
Gold Cup (F) 1958
Ivory Fashion (F) 1959
Saratoga (F) 1964
Apricot Nectar (F) 1966
Gay Princess (F) 1967
Gene Boerner (F) 1969
First Prize (HT) 1970

* * * *

Boerner hybrids chosen as Rose of the Year:

Americana (HT)
Hawaii (HT)
Mexicana (HT)
Polynesian Sunset (HT)

* * * *

Roses hybridized by Boerner, listed alphabetically, with year of introduction:

Aloha (Cl HT) 1949
Americana (HT) 1961
America's Junior Miss (F) 1964
Amy Vanderbilt (F) 1956
Aperitif (F) 1970
Apricot Nectar (F) 1965
Arlene Francis (HT) 1957

Arpege (HT) 1962
Aruba Caribe (HT) 1968
Balinese (HT) 1963
Ballet (HT) 1947
Bermudiana (HT) 1966
Betsy McCall (F) 1956
Bonnie Pink (F) 1964
Bridal Veil (F) 1954
Bridal Pink (F) 1967
Brilliance (F) 1958
Bronze Masterpiece (HT) 1960
Brownie (F) 1959
Calypso (F) 1957
Canadian Centennial (F) 1965
Cape Coral (HT) 1964
Caroline Emmons (F) 1962
Castanet (F) 1960
Chacita (F) 1947
Chatter (F) 1947
Chic (F) 1953
Contentment (HT) 1956
Coolness (F) 1958
Coral Dawn (L Cl) 1953
Coral Gem (F) 1958
Coral Glo (F) 1960
Coral Princess (F) 1965
Coral Sunset (HT) 1966
Crown Jewel (F) 1964
Crystal White (HT) 1965
Dawn Mist (F) 1962
Delightful Pink (F) 1958
Demure (F) 1952
Diamond Jubilee (HT) 1947
Diplomat (HT) 1962
Distinct (F) 1953
Dixie Belle (HT) 1963
Elaine (HT) 1951
Electra (HT) 1968
Ernie Pyle (HT) 1946
Faberge (F) 1969
Fair Lady (HT) 1959

Fashion (F) 1949
Fashion, Climbing (Cl F) 1951
Fashionette (F) 1958
Favorita (HT) 1954
Firecracker (F) 1959
Fireflame (F) 1954
Fire Opal (F) 1955
First Federal (HT) 1965
First Federal Gold (HT) 1967
First Prize (HT) 1970
Frankfurt am Main (F) 1960
Garnette Supreme (F) 1954
Gay Heart (F) 1951
Gay Princess (F) 1967
Geranium Red (F) 1947
Gene Boerner (F) 1969
Ginger (F) 1962
Girl Scout (F) 1961
Glacier (F) 1952
Gold Cup (F) 1957
Golden Chalice (HT) 1960
Golden Fleece (F) 1955
Golden Garnette (F) 1960
Golden Glamour (F) 1951
Golden Lustre (HT) 1964
Golden Masterpiece (HT) 1954
Golden Salute (HT) 1963
Goldie (F) 1958
Goldilocks (F) 1945
Hawaii (HT) 1960
Hildegarde (HT) 1946
Holiday (F) 1948
Honey Gold (F) 1956
Ivory Fashion (F) 1958
Jiminy Cricket (F) 1954
Jingles (F) 1956
John F. Kennedy (HT) 1965
Kate Smith (HT) 1954
Katherine T. Marshall (HT) 1943
Lavender Charm (HT) 1964
Lavender Garnette (F) 1958

Lavender Pinocchio (F) 1948
Lavender Princess (F) 1959
Lodestar (HT) 1953
Mademoiselle (F) 1950
Mandarin (F) 1951
Ma Perkins (F) 1952
Masquerade (F) 1949
Mayday (F) 1957
Medley (HT) 1962
Mexicana (HT) 1966
Minx (F) 1955
Miss Liberty (L Cl) 1956
Misty Gold (F) 1954
Mme. Henri Bonnet (HT) 1948
Moonlight Sonata (HT) 1965
Morning Dawn (L Cl) 1955
New Yorker (HT) 1947
New Yorker, Climbing (HT Cl) 1951
Nobility (HT) 1961
Noweta (F) 1960
Orange Mist (F) 1957
Orange-Red Supreme (F) 1958
Orange Sweetheart (F) 1952
Orchid Masterpiece (HT) 1960
Pageant (HT) 1953
Pan America (HT) 1941
Parade (L Cl) 1953
Party Doll (F) 1958
Peaceful (HT) 1956
Peach Glow (F) 1960
Peggy Newton (F) 1957
Peppermint (F) 1964
Pigmy Gold (F) 1953
Pigmy Lavender (F) 1961
Pigmy Red (F) 1953
Pink-A-Boo (F) 1961
Pink Chiffon (F) 1956
Pink Cloud (L Cl) 1952
Pink Duchess (HT) 1959
Pink Garnette (F) 1951
Pink Glory (HT) 1960

Pink Glow (HT) 1951
Pink Puff (F) 1965
Polynesian Sunset (HT) 1965
Princess White (F) 1956
Queenie (F) 1962
Red Emblem (F) 1958
Red Pinocchio (F) 1947
Red Spice (F) 1958
Red Wings (F) 1958
Revelry (HT) 1958
Sarah Coventry (F) 1956
Saratoga (F) 1963
Satinglo (F) 1954
Saud al Awwal (HT) 1958
Seneca Queen (HT) 1965
Serenade (HT) 1949
Seventeen (F) 1959
Sonnet (HT) 1961
Sonora (F) 1962
Spanish Sun (F) 1966
Spartan (F) 1955
Spice (F) 1954
Starbright (HT) 1962
Stark Whitecap (F) 1959
Summer Frost (F) 1962
Summertime (HT) 1957
Sunset Glory (HT) 1947
Sunset Jubilee (HT) 1973
Sweet Caress (F) 1958
Tam-Tam (F) 1961
Tea Time (F) 1960
Teenager (F) 1958
The Farmer's Wife (F) 1962
Tiara (F) 1960
Timmie Arkles (F) 1954
Tommy Bright (F) 1961
Twilight (HT) 1955
Valiant (HT) 1948
Vin Rosé (HT) 1969
Vogue (F) 1951
White Bouquet (F) 1956

White Demure (F) 1952
White Garnette (F) 1952
White Jewel (F) 1957
White Pinocchio (F) 1950
White Masterpiece (HT) 1969
White Queen (F) 1959
Yellow Gold (HT) 1957
Yellow Pinocchio (F) 1949
Yellow Sweetheart (F) 1952
Zorina (F) 1963

(HT — Hybrid Tea; F — Floribunda; Cl — Climber; L Cl — Large Flowered Climber)

* * * *

In 1971, 441 different varieties of roses won some sort of honors at the nineteen leading rose shows in the United States and Canada. In a tabulation prepared for *The American Rose Magazine* by the Golden Triangle Rose Society of Southeast Texas, one of Boerner's posthumous prize winners scored more points than any other hybrid tea.

On the basis of six points for the best rose of each type, five for second best, and four for third best, his First Prize received a total of 295 points, compared to 178 points for Royal Highness and 142 for Peace.

Six of Boerner's roses ranked among the top twenty floribundas in the 1971 shows, including the Gene Boerner, Ivory Fashion, Fashion, Vogue, Saratoga, and Ginger. Four of his roses which were ranked among twenty grandifloras were also mentioned — Apricot Nectar, Mexicana, Polynesian Sunset, and Gay Princess.

Photo and Illustration Credits

Alfred L. Boerner Botanical Gardens, Milwaukee, Wisconsin
112

Boerner Family Archives
(v), 17, 24, 29, 31, 35, 40, 59, 73,76, 101, 113, 118, 119, 121,
156, Jacket

National Geographic Society, Washington, D. C.
63, 149

Muriel Orans, Horticultural Photography, Corvallis, Oregon
87, 107, 123, 127, 143, 157, 167, 175, 179, 185

JoAnna Poehlmann, Milwaukee, Wisconsin
Jacket Design

Edw. A. Rappold Collection, Cedarburg, Wisconsin
11, 13, 22

State Historical Society of Wisconsin, Madison, Wisconsin 8

Numbers in italics indicate illustrations. ESB *refers to Eugene S. Boerner.*

GENERAL INDEX

ROSE INDEX